T0374364

Data, Systems, and Society

Harnessing the power of data and artificial intelligence (AI) methods to tackle complex societal challenges requires transdisciplinary collaborations across academia, industry, and government. In this compelling book, Munther A. Dahleh, founder of the Institute for Data, Systems, and Society (IDSS) at the Massachusetts Institute of Technology, offers a blueprint for researchers, professionals, and institutions to create approaches to problems of high societal value using innovative, holistic, data-driven methods.

Drawing on his experience at IDSS and knowledge of similar initiatives elsewhere, Dahleh describes in clear, non-technical language how statistics, data science, information and decision systems, and social and institutional behavior intersect across multiple domains. He illustrates key concepts with real-life examples from optimizing transportation to making healthcare decisions during pandemics to understanding the media's impact on elections and revolutions. Dahleh also incorporates crucial concepts such as robustness, causality, privacy, and ethics and shares key lessons learned about transdisciplinary education and about unintended consequences of AI and algorithmic systems.

Munther A. Dahleh is William Coolidge Professor of Electrical Engineering and Computer Science and Founding Director of the Institute for Data, Systems, and Society at the Massachusetts Institute of Technology. He is well known for his seminal contributions to the foundations of the field of decisions under uncertainty, impacting several application domains including transportation systems, power grids, and social, economic, and financial networks. He is a four-time recipient of the IEEE CSS George S. Axelby Outstanding Paper Award for papers in the *IEEE Transactions on Automatic Control* and the 1993 recipient of the Eckman Award for outstanding control engineers under 35.

"I'm often asked by students what they should be studying in the modern era, and my standard response for some years has been 'control theory, economics, and statistics.' Munther Dahleh has been a living embodiment of this blend for as long as I have known him, in this book one accompanies Munther on his very fine adventure in bringing an entire institution into the fold. I hope and expect that many people will read this book, including future historians."

— Michael I. Jordan, *University of California, Berkeley*

"Munther Dahleh's breadth of knowledge is showcased in this discussion that ranges from the history of AI to the building of the world's preeminent institute of data science. Munther provides fascinating insights on the challenges, promise, and successes of using data to improve societies, and delivers a must-read for everyone from budding data scientists to policymakers and institution builders."

— Matthew O. Jackson, *Stanford University*

Data, Systems, and Society

Harnessing AI for Societal Good

Munther A. Dahleh

Massachusetts Institute of Technology

CAMBRIDGE
UNIVERSITY PRESS

CAMBRIDGE
UNIVERSITY PRESS

Shaftesbury Road, Cambridge CB2 8EA, United Kingdom

One Liberty Plaza, 20th Floor, New York, NY 10006, USA

477 Williamstown Road, Port Melbourne, VIC 3207, Australia

314–321, 3rd Floor, Plot 3, Splendor Forum, Jasola District Centre, New Delhi – 110025, India

103 Penang Road, #05–06/07, Visioncrest Commercial, Singapore 238467

Cambridge University Press is part of Cambridge University Press & Assessment, a department of the University of Cambridge.

We share the University's mission to contribute to society through the pursuit of education, learning and research at the highest international levels of excellence.

www.cambridge.org

Information on this title: www.cambridge.org/9781009446198
DOI: 10.1017/9781009446174

First published 2025

Cover image: Sculpture by Jaume Plensa "Alchemist," 2010. 196.85 in. × 141.73 in. × 125.98 in. (500 cm × 360 cm × 320 cm). Stainless steel, white enamel paint. © 2024 Artists Rights Society (ARS), New York / VEGAP, Madrid. Photo credit: John Parrillo.

A catalogue record for this publication is available from the British Library

Library of Congress Cataloging-in-Publication Data
NAMES: Dahleh, Munther A., author.
TITLE: Data, systems, and society : harnessing AI for societal good / Munther A. Dahleh, Massachusetts Institute of Technology.
DESCRIPTION: Cambridge, United Kingdom ; New York, NY, USA : Cambridge University Press, 2025. | Includes bibliographical references and index.
IDENTIFIERS: LCCN 2024045806 (print) | LCCN 2024045807 (ebook) | ISBN 9781009446198 (hardback) | ISBN 9781009446167 (paperback) | ISBN 9781009446174 (epub)
SUBJECTS: LCSH: Technological innovations–Social aspects. | Technology–Social aspects. | Artificial intelligence–Social aspects.
CLASSIFICATION: LCC HM846 .D35 2025 (print) | LCC HM846 (ebook) | DDC 303.48/34–dc23/eng/20250117
LC record available at https://lccn.loc.gov/2024045806
LC ebook record available at https://lccn.loc.gov/2024045807

ISBN 9-781-009-44619-8 Hardback
ISBN 9-781-009-44616-7 Paperback

CONTENTS

PREFACE

When Problems Get Real

Metropolitan Boston, where I happen to live and work, consistently ranks among the worst areas in the US for traffic congestion. In its 2015 report, "Unclogging America's Arteries: Prescriptions for America's Highways," the American Highway Users Alliance estimated that on one infamous two-mile stretch of Boston's Central Artery, drivers expended nearly two million extra gallons of gasoline, wasted more than two million hours, and cost the economy roughly $58 million in lost productivity during a 12-month period. Why? Because the Central Artery features one of the worst highway bottlenecks in the country.

Boston is far from alone in experiencing such dismal traffic consequences. The "2019 Urban Mobility Report" published by the Texas A&M Transportation Institute found that our nation's congestion problems caused 8.8 billion hours of travel delays, wasted 3.3 billion gallons of fuel, and tallied $179 billion of total congestion costs in 2017. Highway and arterial designs, mass transit options, traffic advisories, toll incentives, and the location and availability of affordable housing all contribute to the problem. Most experts agree, however, that any combination of remedies in these areas is likely to bring only modest reductions in congestion-related losses.

What Congestion Has to Do with Data Science

I bring up rush-hour traffic because complicated practical problems of this kind changed my career arc. I started in academia as an electrical engineer and applied mathematician obsessed with the field of learning and decision theory. After joining the MIT faculty in 1987, however, I began to interact more with domain experts – in aerospace and automotive design, for example – and to work on some real-world applications related to my research. Unsurprisingly, space applications, autonomy, and hybrid cars are jam-packed with compelling control problems. My research group, which convenes under the banner "Decisions Under Uncertainty," was a great fit for collaborations in these and other engineering-related domains.

Mitigating vehicular congestion is fascinating to people like us because, increasingly, it is less a physical infrastructure challenge and more a data and networked decisions conundrum. Constructing more or wider roads – which does not solve congestion problems – will be less efficacious going forward than assembling a robust database of real-time information about behaviors and consequences that occur when you and your fellow commuters take to the road. How do you decide when to leave the house or whether to change lanes as traffic clogs? Could you make everyone's drive time shorter if you traveled at an agreed-upon optimal average speed? What are the individual and collective effects of your decisions? How effectively can private and public information mitigate congestion if given to every driver? Such variables can be quantified and the consequences mapped using the analytical methods of contemporary information and decision systems, statistics, and data science.

My growing interest in distributed and networked decisions – think power grids, transportation systems, and financial and social networks – and the interconnections between those systems and human behavior caused me to reassess the relevance of my research. Addressing problems with real and widespread consequences for individuals, communities, businesses, and entire societies drew me out of my disciplinary silo and into transdisciplinary collaborations with domain experts across academia and industry. Along the way, my colleagues and I were offered the opportunity to organize the immense scientific, engineering, humanities, and social science resources of MIT to tackle problems of high societal value using innovative, holistic, data-driven methodologies. The story of our collective journey is the story of the MIT Institute for Data, Systems, and Society (IDSS). As of 2023, we'd been at this for nearly a decade, and I'm happy to say that colleagues at other institutions have developed similar initiatives during that time. A global community of researchers, scholars, and practitioners is taking shape.

Pronouns: An Expression of Community

Before I launch into the main narrative of this book, I'd like to say a word about pronouns. During the writing process, I found myself instinctively defaulting to the first-person plural pronoun "we." My astute editor asked the obvious question, "Who are 'we?'"

For the most part, the ideas and examples in this book are not mine alone. Rather, they arise from years – even decades – of ruminations, conversations, explorations, and innovations among a worldwide community of scholars, researchers, and practitioners across every discipline and endeavor working to improve the lot of humankind. I wanted to express that sense of common cause. The more of us who believe that we all are in this together, the greater chance we have of developing solutions to urgent challenges that will benefit diverse communities, societies, and the planet. This is the outcome we are seeking in our collective journey toward transdisciplinary thinking and practice.

1 THE PITFALLS, PROMISES, AND CHALLENGES OF DATA

Scientific inquiry has always depended on data and various manifestations of data science. The nature of that reliance, however, has metamorphosed dramatically in the twenty-first century. An unprecedented quantity and breadth of information, the ability to share data efficiently among disciplines, ever-expanding computational power, and the democratization of algorithms across domains continue to revolutionize the scientific landscape.

Still largely absent, though, are systematic approaches to using big data to solve the most urgent societal challenges across multiple domains. This book chronicles initiatives underway at the Massachusetts Institute of Technology (MIT) and elsewhere to address that deficit. Our goal in this book is to share key lessons we've learned through the launch of a new transdiscipline of Data, Systems, and Society that applies pioneering technologies to complex challenges. In doing so, we hope to encourage academicians, practitioners, students, and funders to join a growing worldwide effort to use data science for societal good.

Our story will touch on key topics in the history of computing, data science, systems thinking, and the social sciences that contribute to the new methodologies and habits of mind needed to solve previously insoluble problems. Along the way, we'll describe the structure and evolution of our new entity as well as some breakthroughs stemming from our new transdiscipline that demonstrate the promise of novel thinking and interventions.

A Seminal Challenge for Data, Systems, and Society

On March 2021, the Kaiser Family Foundation (KFF) published an analysis of the demographic characteristics of individuals who were vaccinated against coronavirus disease 2019 (COVID-19) throughout the US between mid-December 2020 and March 1, 2021. Citing Centers for Disease Control and Prevention (CDC) data, the report featured two alarming findings related to equity. Of those who had received at least one dose of the vaccine, 65% were White, 9% Hispanic, 7% Black, 5% Asian, 2% American Indian or Alaska Native, fewer than 1% were Native Hawaiian or Other Pacific Islander, and 13% reported mixed or other race.

This was troubling because, as had been noted in a December 2020 KFF report by Samantha Artiga and Jennifer Kates "preventing racial disparities in the uptake of COVID-19 vaccines will be important to help mitigate the disproportionate impacts of the virus for people of color and prevent widening racial health disparities going forward." And yet, KFF analysis of 41 states showed a consistent pattern – Black and Hispanic individuals were receiving smaller shares of vaccinations compared to their shares of infections, deaths, and their percentages of the total population.

Even more worrisome was the revelation that race/ethnicity was known for only slightly more than half (54%) of those who had received at least one dose. The aggregate concerns raised by KFF include not only disparities in vaccination rates but also the extent to which gaps, limitations, and in data collection were limiting the ability of policymakers to assemble a complete picture of who was and was not getting vaccinated. The bright side of KFF's reporting was that those crucial gaps in the data – and the attendant inequities – were brought to light during the early days of vaccine distribution in the US when mitigation and correction could be pursued productively. Efforts to obtain more targeted data are definitely a must if we are to address such disparities.

Bigger Doesn't Always Mean Better

Data always have been the key to scientific discovery. But the collection and analysis of data, in and of itself, does not guarantee results. Misperceptions, misunderstandings, and mistakes often can be traced back to flawed data sets – poor sampling, inconsistent collection or reporting, overly narrow investigation of phenomena, just to name a few root causes of "dirty" data. Reliance on such data can unwittingly prejudice observations and conclusions and provide the rationale for inadequate or counterproductive policy initiatives. Still worse are scenarios in which relevant data are suppressed, intentionally misrepresented or manipulated, or selectively curated to serve the predetermined objectives of the data collector or analyzer.

Unfortunately, so-called big data hasn't yielded the solution to these potential pitfalls. Simply collecting massive amounts of data doesn't guarantee that you will have the specific types of information you need to solve the particular problem you are working on. The CDC vaccination data cited at the beginning of this chapter is just one example of how a very large data set can have limited utility for decision-makers in the midst of a crisis. Policies based on data that underrepresents key segments of the population run the risk of being ineffective at best and counterproductive at worst.

The sheer volume of data we are collecting about almost everything also has the potential to make reliable data-driven decisions impossible. Often, the breadth and depth of information at our disposal far outweigh our brain's ability to account for every data point and potential trend line in a coherent and empowering way. Machines may do this better as long as they are fed with the appropriate data. As is the case with big data circa 2024, we have a lot of data about many things but not enough data about any one particular thing we need to understand deeply. And the new mathematical methods we are perpetually inventing – artificial intelligence (AI) and machine learning (ML) being prime examples from the early twenty-first century – continue to have their own limitations and blind spots. Large language models (LLMs), such as Bard and ChatGPT, are trained on millions of parameters of deep neural networks (DNNs). Much of that data is unlabeled or partially labeled, which can produce good results across many tasks but cannot deliver precise results in the majority of tasks.

As the number of individual users on social platforms such as Facebook grows into multi-billions, so does the cache of data being gleaned from social networks. Such data sets, however, are not collected methodically, are generally unlabeled, and lack consequential information about individual nodes. Those characteristics complicate the task of making causal inferences that would assist researchers and decision-makers with policy development and problem-solving. The field of high-dimensional statistics has contributed many useful low-dimensional models that filter out noisy and irrelevant data, but the speed at which large and messy data sets grow will continue to challenge us for the foreseeable future.

Statistics: A Definition

Statistics is the practice or science of collecting and analyzing numerical data in large quantities and then using that data to make inferences about a whole population based on representative samples. This involves transforming data into models to aid in decision-making processes such as prediction and regulation. Statistics plays a fundamental role in the process of scientific discovery and serves as a foundation for many quantitative fields. It also comprises the field of statistical learning theory, which addresses essential questions related to learning models from data. In linear regression, for example, a simple linear model is fitted to one or more data sets to predict or classify data points. The theory provides a probabilistic framework to assess how well the model represents reality, considering aspects such as sample complexity and model evaluation. ML is founded on statistical learning theory and often refers to unstructured learning problems.

Timescales and Shortfalls

Often, the data we need and obtain occur on multiple, even divergent, time scales and lack the dynamism of the real-world phenomena from which they are drawn. Such challenges help explain why the task of optimizing the US electrical grid has confounded public- and private-sector organizations for decades. Operating costs and pricing, human behavior (demand and usage patterns), the performance capabilities and limitations of technologies, and the inherently deliberate nature of decision-making institutions function on vastly different time scales across broad geographic areas. And the types of data we gather from those phenomena often fail to conform to a single analytical tool or methodology.

If too much data has its drawbacks, too little data is even more unfortunate. As we saw from the example at the beginning of this chapter, well-intentioned policymakers can be stymied from drawing actionable conclusions when the data on hand fail to fully account for key components of the problem. Phenomena and systems that are characterized based on small and/or narrow data sets also are much more easily misrepresented or manipulated for nefarious purposes.

Another data scarcity pitfall arises when we try to measure and analyze rare, but critical, failures in networked systems such as power grids, financial markets, and transportation systems. Small, idiosyncratic disruptions occasionally cascade into major breakdowns. Because those events are infrequent, we have limited information with which to build the data-driven predictive models we need. The 2021 paper "Cascading Risks: Understanding the 2021 Winter Blackout in Texas" by Joshua W. Busby and nine coauthors about the collapse of Texas' power generation capabilities in February 2021 highlighted our need to understand the mechanisms behind such catastrophes. If we correctly analyze those mechanisms, we may be able to make predictions about potential future failures with much less data. We must understand the underlying phenomena generating the data in order to make reliable conclusions or decisions.

Causality

Back in the days before the data science revolution, I would introduce new students to my research group by walking them around our lab space and showing them where they would be sitting. I often used the opportunity to joke that if the new student agreed to sit at a particular desk, they were guaranteed to graduate. My evidence? Every previous student who sat at that desk had graduated. Most new students would laugh at my quip and recognize the absurdity of my argument. On rare occasions, though, a student would accept my rationale at face value – which left me worrying that they didn't understand the difference between causality and correlation.

Nowadays, the causality/correlation distinction is fairly well understood in everyday contexts (e.g., a CNN news broadcast), and it is ubiquitous in many scientific and technological endeavors. This spans a variety of fields, including drug design, recommendation systems, and economic policy.

A fun illustration of causality and the presence of a confounding factor involves ice cream and sunburns. If we examine data on ice cream consumption and sunburns, we may observe a seemingly inexplicable correlation that suggests that eating a frozen dairy dessert and getting over-tanned are related. Once you incorporate a third variable such as going to the beach, however, the correlation makes more sense. We can deduce the probability that eating ice cream and experiencing sunburns, when conditioned on going to the beach, are simply independent of one another.

Causality plays a crucial role in recommendation systems, with these systems serving as a primary example of extracting causal information from observational data. When examining sparse customer ratings data from Netflix, the challenge arises in assessing a customer's interest in a particular movie for recommendation. For instance, can we determine if customer A is interested in movie X based on their observed behavior?

Nearest neighbor methods attempt to address this by identifying another customer B, who has rated past movies similarly to customer A and has also given a high rating to movie X. The proximity argument is then used to infer that customer A may be interested in movie X.

However, there are several caveats to this approach. First, it may be challenging to find a single person who is highly similar to customer A. This challenge has led to the development of synthetic control groups, where a collection of individuals collectively approximates the behavior of customer A. More importantly, the absence of a rating for movie X from customer A may not be random; it could be due to a lack of interest. This introduces the possibility that the absence of a rating is confounded by some other unmeasurable variable. Consequently, it becomes challenging to confidently ascertain customer A's interest in movie X.

Drug designers cannot bring a product to market without establishing causation through randomized clinical trials (RCTs) and control groups that demonstrate the causes and effects of a drug. To mitigate the influence of unknown confounders, two populations of randomly selected subjects are created. The randomness ensures that these groups are not biased in specific ways, such as being composed entirely of women or individuals of a particular age.

In the trial, one group is administered the drug, while the other group receives a placebo. The effects are measured by calculating the average outcome within the first group and comparing it to the average outcomes of the second group. This comparison yields what is known as the average treatment effect, providing a reliable assessment of the drug's causal impact while controlling for potential confounding variables.

At the random population level, RCTs are instrumental in determining whether there is a measurable difference between applying the drug and not applying it. However, despite these insights, we still face uncertainty at the individual level. In other words, we cannot definitively predict what will happen if a specific person who initially received a placebo is later given the drug.

The personalized treatment effect represents a deeper layer of causality that is of significant interest. While RCTs may contain information that allows for the assessment of this effect, it necessitates a more in-depth analysis of the data. Understanding how the drug interacts with an individual's unique characteristics, health conditions, and other factors requires a more nuanced examination beyond the broad conclusions drawn at the population level. This personalized treatment effect is crucial for tailoring medical interventions to individuals and optimizing healthcare outcomes.

Causality from observational data is the holy grail of statistics, and one that has a profound impact on how we explain data. But running experiments can be expensive and impractical, so we often find ourselves short of data that demonstrate causality. Human health initiatives – think gene therapy or finding a cure for Lyme disease – are notoriously difficult to study in live subjects, for example. Because the search for cures must persist in the face of data scarcity, we must increase and enhance our ability to examine mechanisms using models in research and development.

When working with purely observational data – including initiatives that don't lend themselves to RCTs – we must devise alternative approaches for determining cause and effect. This is often the case in econometrics when researchers construct instrumental variables and synthetic control groups that limit potential dependence on confounders. My colleague Alberto Abadie's article "Using Synthetic Controls: Feasibility, Data Requirements, and Methodological Aspects" is a good reference for those who want to explore the topic in detail.

We see synthetic controls at work in contemporary American life when the board of governors of the US Federal Reserve System (the Fed) grapples with where to set interest rates. Historically, policymakers have observed that raising interest rates can produce a measurable effect on reducing inflation. But observational data are not free of confounders. If the Fed is buying more federally issued bonds at the same time it is raising interest rates, for example, the resulting effect on inflation cannot be attributed solely to higher rates. Full-scale live experiments on the US economy are out of the question, so the governors must do the best they can with observational data and statistical modeling to establish causal relationships.

The Challenge of Interconnected Systems

Interconnections among subsystems create very different dependencies and phenomena from systems in isolation – though we often take these interconnections for granted. When we are sailing along smoothly at 30,000 feet on a commercial flight between Atlanta and Boston, we take it for granted that the plane is engineered to travel safely between the two cities in the hands of a skilled pilot (or more likely autopilot). Even if we are aware of the complex guidance and decision-making systems that assist pilots, we seldom think about the interconnection between the airplane and the global control systems that coordinate flight paths, takeoffs, and landings. Disconnecting an airborne commercial airliner from this complex system could be catastrophic, and attempting to understand the workings of the global aviation industry apart from this system would be futile.

Those interconnections can also result in cascaded failures, such as what happened in 2016 when Atlanta experienced a three-inch snowfall (a storm that Boston residents would consider negligible). As a result of that single weather event, air traffic experts projected three-hour delays for certain flights leaving Los Angeles. We all understand that delays in airports are interlinked and that delays at Atlanta International Airport could result in cascaded delays at LAX. But why were the flights in Atlanta delayed in the first place?

Airport operators in Atlanta certainly have the necessary equipment to remove three inches of snow from the runways without interrupting takeoffs and landings. The city of Atlanta, by contrast, does not invest in infrastructure for snow removal at the same scale because three-inch snowstorms are rare events. When the 2016 storm congested Atlanta-area roads, pilots and crew members were unable to reach the airport in time for their scheduled flights (despite the availability of transit to the airport). The interconnections and dependencies between ground and air transportation were the true cause of the systemic failure in airline travel that day. We'll dive deeper into interconnections, feedback, and complexity later in this book.

I'll have more to say in upcoming chapters about the strategies we employ at the Institute for Data, Systems, and Society (IDSS) – abstraction, dissecting mechanisms of failure, statistical analyses, causality, and mapping human and institutional behavior through the lens of social sciences – to zero in on viable solutions to complex, data-rich challenges. Before I launch into an overview of our transdisciplinary methodologies, however, we must consider the issues of privacy, bias, and fairness in data collection and use.

Exploring the Limits of Privacy

In March 2021, journalist Kashmir Hill reported in *New York Times Magazine* that a little-known company called Clearview AI had created a database with three billion images of people. The photos came from social media, employment sites, YouTube, and Venmo – all part of the public web – and included links to the sites where each of the images originated. When the activities of Clearview were first exposed by journalists, several companies (Facebook, Google, and LinkedIn among them) pursued cease-and-desist actions, all of which failed.

The existence of such web-scraping technologies was not, by itself, newsworthy. The startling aspects of the revelations were the scale of the human image base (many times larger than similar products used by law enforcement at that time), the fact that individuals depicted had no idea their images had been collected, and the list of people and organizations accessing the technology. According to Hill's reporting, *BuzzFeed* leaked an inventory of users that included Bank of America, the NBA, and a billionaire investor in Clearview who used the image base to ID his daughter's dinner date who was otherwise unknown to him.

Although this example represents only a tiny portion of personal information being collected without our knowledge, it highlights well the extent to which individual privacy has been compromised by massive data-collection activities. As we race ahead to solve pressing societal challenges with rich new information sources, must we accept the losses of personal information we've already sustained and seek to limit the pitfalls? Or should we be fighting to claw back some of the privacy we've unwittingly sacrificed? The push and pull implicit in these questions reflect a societal debate that may never be fully resolved.

Privacy Gains and Losses

One reason we are unlikely to return to pre-digital-age notions of privacy is that people simply aren't inclined to do so. A January 2019 survey by the Center for Data Innovation found that 58% of Americans would give sensitive personal data – such as location, medical, and biometric – in exchange for immediate or long-term benefits. Expected ROIs ranged from increased convenience (easier logins, free navigation assistance, etc.) to cures that might improve the health and well-being of ourselves and others.

On the flip side, the Pew Research Center reported in November 2019 that 66% of Americans considered the potential risks of allowing governmental entities to collect their personal data to outweigh the benefits. Wariness was even greater (81% expressed an aversion) when applied to private companies. Yet businesses forge ahead – Amazon, for example, began requiring its delivery drivers to submit to AI surveillance of their locations, movements, and biometric data in 2021 – while US regulatory bodies seem to be frozen in place like the proverbial deer in the headlights.

People are conflicted. They want to believe that big data can benefit both the individual and society without subjecting either to high levels of risk or intrusion. Those of us who work with and conduct research into data and systems believe we can achieve this balance, but we have a lot of convincing to do before we can gain the necessary buy-in from the general public.

Data Collection, Biases, and Algorithmic Fairness

While many of us view data as key to solving our most complex challenges, it also has created seemingly intractable, society-wide problems. One of the earliest and most notorious misapplications of data was the introduction of racial categorizations into the US Census in the mid-nineteenth century. A substantial majority of researchers today agree that the genetic argument for those categorizations was tenuous at best – the differences in genetic structures are continuous and far from belonging in distinct, enumerated clusters. Phenotypes in genetic structures do not differentiate based on these divisions, and sociologists assert that racial structures emerged from social relations that the Census categories reinforced. My colleague, MIT Chancellor Melissa Nobles, covered this topic well in her book *Shades of Citizenship: Race and the Census in Modern Politics*.

Many far-reaching public policies – voting rights, housing, healthcare, biometrics, policing, and crime prevention, to name a few – have relied on these categories and reinforced patterns of structural bias and individual racism. Over time, such policies reinforced divisions and created socially defined races that favored some groups and disadvantaged others. Decades of redlining by home mortgage lenders, for example, prevented Black borrowers from buying property in higher-value zip codes. As Chat Travieso observed in "A Nation of Walls: The Overlooked History of Race Barriers in the United States," the practice created a self-fulfilling cycle that prevented the accumulation of generational wealth and widened the wealth gap between Black and White Americans.

In recent decades, patterns of surveillance data collection in predominantly Black neighborhoods have created another self-fulfilling cycle of bias. Biased assumptions about higher crime rates in Black neighborhoods were used to justify greater surveillance. Closer observation resulted in more arrests, and the data were used to justify even more surveillance. Now you have a data set showing that more arrests occur in predominantly Black than in predominantly White neighborhoods, lending further credence to biased policing and crime prevention policies. Readers will find a rigorous analysis of those counterfactual effects in the 2017 paper "Counterfactual Fairness" by Matt J. Kusner, Joshua Loftus, Chris Russell, and Ricardo Silva. When fed into ML algorithms, data showing higher arrest records generate predictions of more crime and justify even more police presence. It should come as no surprise that the policies and practices borne of this biased data collection and analysis actually have diminished public safety in affected areas.

Members of the data science community are diligently seeking to bring fairness to algorithmic processes by applying methods that correct for biased data sets. "Racially unaware" algorithms attempt to remove all references to race from data, but externalities in data sets complicate this process and leave many unconvinced of the efficacy of this approach. A different method known as statistical parity (SP) compares algorithmic decisions across two or more categories of people to identify comparability – or lack thereof – in assessments of risk, false positives, false negatives, and other factors. Unfortunately, SP has proven inconsistent in detecting bias when applied to complex, real-world systems. For a detailed tutorial on how fair-minded ML practitioners can better serve marginalized and oppressed populations, I recommend "The Fairness Field Guide: Perspectives from Social and Formal Sciences" by Alycia N. Carey and Xintao Wu.

Making Data Count

On any given day, business management newsletters and periodicals publish more advice on monetizing data than the average person can read in 24 hours. Many offer some version of "You're collecting all this data, now here's how you can use it to boost profits." That plethora of guidance speaks to the fact that accumulating massive amounts of data became a minor obsession for many organizations long before their leaders had any idea what to do with that information.

Facebook and Google, of course, led the way in converting big data into cash flow, with Amazon hitting its data-monetization stride in the late 2010s. Robert J. Shapiro, former undersecretary of commerce in the Clinton administration, and Siddhartha Aneja, a policy analyst at the Georgetown Center on Poverty & Inequality, reported in 2019 that Amazon appears to have more than doubled its earnings on user data between 2016 and 2018. The pair also calculated that Facebook profited from users' personal information to the tune of $35.2 billion in 2018 – 63% of Facebook's total earnings that year.

Clearly, the pitfalls of big data discussed earlier in this chapter aren't preventing companies from using our personal information to haul in a great deal of money. I'm not suggesting that we should – or could – dramatically restrict data monetization, provided those activities meet widely accepted societal standards for consent, transparency, and equity. I will argue, however, that boosting the bottom lines of businesses is far from the greatest societal benefit we can reap from big data.

We know, for example, that heterogeneous, dynamic data on climate, soil conditions, and disease outbreaks can be just as life-changing for small- to medium-sized potato farmers in Peru as deep public health data were to the entire world during the COVID-19 pandemic. Hundreds of projects with similar societal objectives are underway throughout the world on any given day, and many thousands more will follow in the coming decades if we can gain peoples' trust that our data-gathering activities are governed by rigorous ethical, inclusive, and respectful guidelines.

At IDSS, we contend that data collection – and the ethics, rationales, and methodologies behind it – are at least as important as the algorithms we devise to analyze the information we gather. Human behaviors and incentives must be carefully accounted for across the full spectrum of applicable populations if we are to create or improve the systems that dominate contemporary life. Climate, food, energy, transportation, healthcare, education, finance, commerce, media, governance, and even our understanding of what it means to be human all stand to be enhanced with broader and more effective uses of data.

At the same time, we must empower individuals to secure their personal information from unnecessary intrusions, unauthorized disclosures, and intentional or unintentional misuse by third parties. If we clearly articulate the problems we are trying to solve and are transparent about how we will use the data we are collecting, I believe we will increase trust among the general public. In doing so, we also will boost individuals' willingness to participate in the types of data-gathering efforts that will yield long-term societal benefits.

The Income-Inequality Debate: Case in Point

Thomas Piketty's influential research, including his seminal work *Capital in the 21st Century*, has heightened global awareness of escalating income inequality. His comprehensive analysis of recent decades in the US exposes a widening gap between the top 1% and the bottom 50% of earners. Between 1980 and 2020, for example, the share of pre-tax income among the lower 50% of earners declined by 9.6%, while the share among the top 1% of earners rose by 8.2%. Piketty attributes this trend to a persistent phenomenon – the growth rate of inherited wealth surpasses earned income during periods of sluggish economic performance. The higher return on capital during those periods perpetuates the concentration of capital and wealth among a privileged few. Factors related to managerial power also contribute to the exacerbation of inequality over time. Piketty argues that mitigating effects of that overall trend in the first half of the twentieth century – wars, industrialization, education, and economic growth – were no more than temporary setbacks to the broader dynamic of rising income inequality that continues to this day.

Piketty proposes a range of governmental interventions to mitigate the widening gap, emphasizing increased taxation for the wealthy (e.g., capital gains and inheritance taxes) as well as intensified efforts to combat tax evasion. He also advocates for substantial social investments in areas such as education, healthcare, and debt cancellation. The effectiveness of these pivotal changes, he asserts, rests on the conclusiveness of the data analysis conducted, underscoring the paramount importance of rigorous and responsible data science.

Piketty's prescriptions, though widely embraced, also have inspired pushback. Gerald Auten from the Office of Taxation at the US Treasury and David Splinter of the Joint Committee on Taxation of the US Congress, for example, contest Piketty's methodology in their article "Income Inequality in the United States: Using Tax Data to Measure Long-Term Trends." They argue that Piketty and collaborators Emmanuel Saez and Gabriel Zucman at the World Inequality Lab may have systematically attributed more wealth to the top 1%, thereby potentially overstating the issue of inequality.

Auten and Splinter contend that the increase in income inequality during recent decades is approximately half the amount estimated by Piketty, Saez, and Zucman. The ongoing debate has evolved through multiple iterations and rebuttals between the two camps, culminating in the 2024 publication of the most recent Auten and Splinter paper in the *Journal of Political Economy*. This scholarly duel highlights the intricacies of data science and emphasizes the critical role methodology plays in deriving accurate and reliable conclusions from economic data. It also underscores the inherent challenges in achieving a data-driven understanding of income inequality, in particular, and of complex socio-economic issues, in general.

The Core of the Debate

One intriguing aspect of the debate between Piketty, Saez, and Zucman on one side and Auten and Splinter on the other is that both camps rely on common data sets for their analyses. Those data sets include information from the Internal Revenue Service, Federal Reserve Board, Bureau of Economic Analysis, and miscellaneous data sets and research that estimate unreported incomes in various ways. The two sides also share a common understanding about the timing of various government interventions that might have impacted some misreported income (e.g., which tax laws affected outcomes when they took effect). The sides agree, as well, that income should be associated with individuals. Despite all that common ground, other factors cause the two camps to diverge.

The Piketty/Saez/Zucman method ranks incomes based on the total amounts reported by tax filers (with jointly reported income split evenly between filers) and then compares the total income of the top 1% to that of the bottom 50% of earners. The Auten/Splinter approach, by contrast, ranks incomes by integrating the number of children in a family and then normalizes income by the unit's size (i.e., dividing by the square root of the number of people). Once ranked, Auten/Splinter assigns the full income (not the normalized one) to its respective grouping.

When you apply the Auten/Splinter approach to a couple married filing jointly with four children and a $500,000 income, the effective income for ranking is $204,124. In contrast, if you apply the Piketty, Saez, and Zucman approach, the effective income for ranking is $250,000. Since after ranking both groups agree that the income for that family unit remains $500,000, the Auten and Splinter approach creates a higher average income for the lower 99% of earners as compared to the Piketty/Saez/Zucman ranking method. By placing higher-income units into lower groups, the Auten and Splinter method effectively reduces the overall calculation of the income gap. As one might expect, the Piketty/Saez/Zucman team rejects that approach and asserts that children and other dependents who are not income earners should be considered part of a consumption model rather than an income distribution model.

Undisclosed Taxable Income

In a related line of inquiry, numerous researchers have examined the complex issue of misreported income that should be – but is not – taxed. Although audit data can provide insights into this aspect of wealth accumulation, it also poses a sophisticated modeling problem. Audits lack randomization and reflect government policies that are grounded in prior beliefs about income-hiding behaviors within certain groups. Those beliefs and behaviors undoubtedly fluctuate whenever tax laws change. As a consequence, researchers in this domain must create estimates of hidden taxable income for various income groups by inputting the data on undeclared income and correcting for biases. Such models must also estimate the percentage of evaders within each group (often referred to as the frequency of evasion).

Both the Piketty/Saez/Zucman and Auten/Splinter camps rely on the same frequency-of-evasion research to quantify and allocate misreported income that should be taxed (i.e., evaded income). Nonetheless, the allocation of evaded income turns out to be the largest driver of differences in income-share estimates between the two camps. Piketty and his collaborators allocate evaded income to each group of taxpayers in proportion to reported income. Auten and Splinter, however, use information about the frequency and magnitude of tax evasion to allocate evaded income to randomly selected filers by reported income group. Both camps then re-rank taxpayers by income to determine the top 1% and bottom 50% of earners. Just as with their divergent approach to income ranking, the Auten/Splinter methodology for tax evasion attributes more generated income for the bottom 99% of taxpayers than the Piketty/Saez/Zucman's approach and produces a narrower gap between the two income groups. While both approaches are sensitive to estimates of unreported income, I contend that the Auten/Splinter approach results in a more granular allocation of evaded income.

Transparency and Data Availability

The intense debate between the opposing income-inequality camps is, in my view, a fine example of the robust scientific discourse we seek to promote within the Data, Systems, and Society domain. Piketty and his collaborators have made their data available to the scientific community to analyze and potentially replicate. They also have acknowledged errors in their work, even as they have defended their overall assumptions and findings. Without such transparency, progress on complex socio-economic challenges would be greatly impeded.

The income-inequality debate highlights the multifaceted nature of analyzing and responding to societal-level problems. Allocating government expenditures in areas such as healthcare, housing, or education, for example, illustrates the need for a consistent and defensible methodology. Accounting for auditing behaviors and trends highlights the need to understand factors that introduce bias into data. And despite many shared assumptions and information, a few key divergences in methodology produced significantly different – and comparably robust – findings. With respect to income inequality, the work has significantly advanced our understanding of the challenge. In a broader sense, the combined efforts of both camps have demonstrated the power and potential of data and systems thinking.

2 A CONFLUENCE OF FIELDS
Some Historical Perspective

I marvel – as do many of my colleagues – at the pace of developments in data science, ML, and AI during the first two decades of the twenty-first century. Given my own wonder at the speed of progress, I certainly understand how the average person may feel that all this dropped out of the sky fully formed. It didn't, of course, and my hope is that a brief recap of key historical milestones in these fields will help us better appreciate the interconnecting factors that produced the current state of affairs. The history of developments can also enable us to understand more clearly the immense potential of future break-throughs in computing power, data science, data abundance, ML, and the development of superior algorithms.

Computing and Big Data: Some Historical Perspective

I take it on faith – and as empirical fact – that problems have solutions and decisions have consequences. Not all solutions and consequences are equal, however, and much of human history can be explained by our quest for better outcomes. We have proved, as a species, to be tireless in our efforts to enhance our problem-solving and decision-making with tools, machines, and methodologies. Contemporary computing technologies are simply the latest, though arguably the most consequential, manifestation of this eternal drive. How is it that these technologies have come to be so dominant in our lives, and why are initiatives such as IDSS important for advancing the academic pursuit of better outcomes?

Consider two simple data points as a measure of our societal journey in computing from the 1950s to the 2020s. In 1953, just as IBM was preparing to manufacture the world's first mass-produced computer (the "650"), approximately 100 computers were functioning on the planet according to some estimates. I haven't been able to verify that number, but even if it's remotely accurate, that's in the range of one computer for every 20–30 million people. By late 2014, several sources put the number of personal computers (PCs) in use around the globe at roughly two billion – one computer for every 3.6 people. And that number doesn't include smartphones and tablets, which are even more plentiful than desktops and laptops and have lots more memory, faster processors, and greater storage capacities than the original IBM 650.

Of course, this simple accounting of existing hardware only hints at how the evolution of computing has transformed our capabilities and dependencies, redefined our economic and social ecosystems, and altered the course of human history. It does illustrate, however, just how dominant computer technologies have become in almost everyone's life. When I reflect on my own journey in computing, I find that certain developments during the last several decades, beginning in the 1960s, are particularly relevant to the creation of IDSS.

The Roots of Mainframe Computers

Analog machines – which measure and process data based on streams of physical input such as light, temperature, or voltage – date back millennia. As long ago as 100 BC, inventors built devices to calculate astronomical positions, solve complex mathematical equations, predict tides, and even aim naval artillery. At the beginning of the modern era, mechanically, hydraulically, and electrically driven computers were developed for fire control and electrical power systems. Because these "network analyzers" were able to handle complex numerical calculations, they were also used by nuclear physicists and structural engineers before and after World War II. One of the first digital-analog vacuum tube computers in this lineage that provided real-time outputs was the Whirlwind I, developed in the Servomechanisms Lab at MIT in the 1940s and 1950s. MIT's Laboratory of Decision Systems (LIDS) – with which I'm proudly affiliated – is a descendant of Project Whirlwind and the lab that gave birth to it.

Analog computers are still in use for specialized applications. Their overall importance, however, started to wane in the second half of the twentieth century. With the development of vacuum tubes, transistors, integrated circuits, and then microprocessors, government- and industry-backed scientists and engineers began to create a new class of general-purpose computers that were faster and more versatile than analog devices. Mass production of these multi-cabinet, multi-central processing unit (CPU) machines – generically referred to as mainframes – ramped up in the 1950s, and mainframes grew to dominate academic and industrial computing in the 1960s and 1970s.

Why Mainframes Matter: First Revolution

The development of mainframes provided the foundation for entire categories of modern computer technologies that we take for granted today – memory storage media, user interfaces, programming languages, discrete transistors, integrated circuits, output and interface devices (i.e., printers, graphic displays, mouses, and trackpads), just to name a few. The unprecedented capabilities of those technologies prompted physicist Howard H. Aiken to quip, "We'll have to think up bigger problems if we want to keep them [computers] busy." Landmark machines such as the Universal Automatic Computer (UNIVAC), Whirlwind, Automatic Computing machine of the Mathematica Center (ARMAC), and ATLAS were developed for tasks ranging from compiling US census data and processing payroll at General Electric to controlling transportation networks (e.g., air and rail traffic) and monitoring America's airborne early warning defense system.

Mainframes also enabled large-scale simulations of complex phenomena such as weather fronts, financial systems, transportation networks, and aerospace flight. These and related hardware capabilities were of particular interest to me in the 1980s as I began my research into control theory and capabilities and limitations of control systems under uncertainty. My PhD thesis adopted a wholly computational perspective in the design of control systems, diverging significantly from the analytical "closed-form" solutions that have traditionally been the focal point of the field. In the decades that followed the invention of mainframe computers, I and my colleagues in electrical engineering, applied mathematics, computer science, and statistics would never be at a loss for bigger and more complex problems to challenge faster and more sophisticated computing capabilities.

Vignette

The era of mainframes undoubtedly launched a paradigm shift in how systems and processes were handled, a time when we crossed the threshold into a world where advances in computing began to move much more rapidly than our ability to adapt to them. This revolution produced, and continues to produce, many unintended consequences that have not been positive for society at large. Many scholars contend, for example, that mainframe computing facilitated racial division in America by helping to statistically codify the now-debunked notion of single-race individuals in the decennial compiling of the US Census. The power of databases, in particular, facilitated racialized data collection that was used to develop racialized – and discriminatory – policies in housing, healthcare access and research, and other areas.

The Turing Test

In the mid-twentieth century, the increasing power (in speed and storage) of mainframe computers triggered profound philosophical and scientific inquiries. One of the most widely recognized voices in the debate was the pioneering mathematician and computer scientist Alan Turing. In 1950, he posed the fundamental question, "Can machines think?" That question, which epitomized what became known as the Turing Test, sparked extensive discussions about the nature of intelligence and the potential of machines.

To answer his famous question, Turing plumbed the depths of predicate calculus and predicate logic, conducting rigorous analyses of formulas and functions. Through his exploration, he arrived at a significant conclusion – neither a Turing Machine nor any other logical method could answer every mathematical question. That insight laid the groundwork for understanding the inherent limitations of formal systems and their applicability to real-world problem-solving. Those limitations, however, did not hinder the development of the technology we refer to as AI that is poised to transform contemporary society.

The Founding Event of AI

In September 1955, mathematicians and engineers John McCarthy, Marvin Minsky, Nathaniel Rochester, and Claude Shannon proposed what would become the founding event for the field of AI, the 1956 Dartmouth Summer Research Project on Artificial Intelligence. The conference convened a small, but enthusiastic, group of scientists and researchers with high hopes for the development of intelligent machines. Unfortunately, the outcomes of the project fell well short of the intent, and the group concluded that achieving true machine intelligence was a far more complex endeavor than initially projected. Despite that overarching disappointment, the participants succeeded in laying the essential groundwork for the development of AI that followed.

In 1963, the Defense Advanced Research Projects Agency (DARPA) launched AI research at MIT. The initiative marked a significant step toward government involvement in AI research that helped accelerate advances in the field. In the early 1970s, MIT Professor Marvin Minsky ignited a surge of excitement and anticipation within the scientific community (and beyond) when he predicted that AI – equivalent to the cognitive abilities of an average human – could be achieved within three to eight years – a somewhat optimistic prediction. The first manifestation of a technology matching Minsky's prediction came in the early 1980s with the creation of "expert systems" by Stanford Professor Edward Feigenbaum. Those systems proliferated rapidly and deeply influenced the AI landscape for the remainder of the decade.

Can Neural Networks Learn Everything?

In parallel with the pioneering work of Turing, Minsky, Feigenbaum, and others, machine learning (ML) researchers were exploring the potential of artificial neural networks (NNs), which also played a key role in the development of AI. That work originated with Canadian psychologist Donald O. Hebb's formulation of the neuronal model in his 1949 book *The Organization of Behavior*. Hebb's model proposed that collections of interconnected neurons could give rise to complex behavior. The concept of interconnected neural units laid the groundwork for understanding how learning and memory might be represented in the human brain. It also set the stage for brain-inspired computational models that can be trained to execute a wide range of tasks.

The Perceptron, introduced by psychologist Frank Rosenblatt in 1957, marked a turning point in the development of NNs. Building on Hebb's 1949 neuronal model, the Perceptron used a simple mathematical model with an associated algorithm to learn a simple binary classifier. A full layer of Perceptrons then incorporated an algorithm for learning a system's parameters and demonstrated the potential pattern recognition and decision-making capabilities of machines. Further research in this vein produced more efficient and powerful multilayer networks, which, in turn, led to the rise of DNNs. The "deep" in DNN refers to the presence of multiple layers hidden between input and output layers. Those deeper architectures facilitated the representation of complex and hierarchical relationships in data and enabled DNNs to excel in various tasks such as image and speech recognition, natural language processing, and more.

In 1950, IBM computer scientist Arthur L. Samuel introduced a computer program capable of playing checkers. Prior to his breakthrough, the vast number of possible states in a game of checkers couldn't be navigated exhaustively by machine. To surmount that difficulty, Samuel employed a scoring mechanism that estimated the probability of winning at each board configuration and guided the program to make strategic moves. He updated these probabilities by having the program play itself. The approach was an early manifestation of reinforcement learning (RL), and it marked a seminal step in the use of algorithms and heuristics to tackle complex decision-making tasks that mimic human decision-making – the genesis of contemporary AI. We note, however, that Samuel did not use NNs for his work.

Progress in ML using NNs and DNNs remained firmly grounded in the realm of statistical learning theory. Considerations related to predictive accuracy, data resilience, and the time complexity associated with the quantity of data necessary for achieving precision were closely intertwined with the capacity to fine-tune multiple parameters of NNs. The domains of high-dimensional statistics and optimization were pivotal in shaping the core of ML progression.

The parallel development of predicate logic, first pursued by Turing and other researchers, as well as the exploration of NNs for ML (by Rosenblatt and others), showcases the diverse avenues of inquiry during the early days of AI. These distinct paths represented contrasting approaches to understanding and building AI. And yet, the progress of ML research was significantly hindered by the physical limitations of computational power and storage capacity at that time. For a decade or more, researchers grappled with the formidable challenges posed by the sheer computational complexity of training and running ML algorithms. How could those dual tracks – rooted in different theoretical approaches – converge in a multidisciplinary field that combined logic, computation, and neuroscience to create the modern landscape of AI and ML? The fields were crying out for a computational hardware and software revolution.

Personal Computers to the Rescue: Second Revolution

I still recall getting my first Apple II PC in 1981. Setting it up was an ordeal worth enduring. Suddenly, I had all the computational power I needed at my disposal. On the PC, I was able to perform all the scientific programming needed for my courses and research, as well as write and edit my undergraduate thesis. Although PCs democratized computation, it was still largely limited to people interested in scientific computing.

Less than a decade later, however, our PCs were connected to the internet. With the development of Mosaic, the World Wide Web, and subsequent web browsers, our personal workstations became tools for both computation and communication. This was the tipping point for the universal adoption of PCs, and we began applying computing capabilities to every aspect of our lives. The advent of networked computers incentivized a new era of distributed computing that has enabled transformative developments in those capabilities.

An "Aloha!" Moment for Computing

I find it fitting that the first great breakthrough in network computing – courtesy of the University of Hawaii in 1971 – bore the name "ALOHAnet." The word "aloha" is commonly understood by non-islanders to mean both "hello" and "goodbye." The metaphor is poignant because one of the most significant technical achievements of ALOHAnet was a method for gatekeeping the communications between satellite-campus "client" machines and the main-campus "hub" machine. In essence, the hub computer at Oahu controlled and verified the beginning and end of transmissions between itself and each of the node computers on the other islands – a sort of hello, goodbye, and hello again mechanism. That system was key to enabling the hub and all client nodes to interact on the same frequency, a key starting point for what we know today as distributed computing, whereby multiple machines at different nodes share resources and computational power to execute one computational task.

You can take the metaphor just a bit further, I think, when you consider what the ALOHAnet breakthrough meant to the evolution of computing. Just as native Hawaiians hold the deeper meaning of aloha to include mutual respect and understanding, so does distributed computing offer the possibility of exchanges of information, ideas, collaborations, and solutions that promote mutual respect and shared progress. Although the second decade of the twenty-first century has revealed some of the dark side of digital information exchange, I would argue that the promise of its demonstrated and potential benefits can outweigh its perils – provided we commit our minds and resources to its upsides.

Why did distributed systems and computing become all the rage? Expense, for one thing. A cluster of networked, low-end computers can often complete high-performance computing tasks less expensively than a single high-end computer. Such systems also tend to be easier to manage and expand, and they offer greater reliability because they don't have a single point of failure. Most important, arguably, was the capability of distributed systems to transmit data collected or produced at one location for processing or analysis at another location using existing and new communications networks – a core characteristic of twenty-first-century computing.

Smart Phone and Cell Tower Coevolution: Third Revolution

If you didn't live through the early days of mobile computing in the early 1980s, you may find it nearly impossible to fathom that display screens on the first laptops (e.g., Osborne 1, Epson HX-20, and Kyocera Kyotronic) were smaller than the average smartphone of 2020 – and only 10–20% of the surface area of those early machines' faceplates. Such devices were mobile in the sense that a person of average strength could carry one from location A to location B, power up, and run a handful of basic software applications (spreadsheets, word processors, calculators, and mail mergers) without being plugged into a power source for some period of time. In most other respects, they bore almost no resemblance to the supercharged, handheld wonders of today.

As cumbersome as those machines would appear to us today, they unquestionably sparked the imagination of the public at large – and ultimately launched a worldwide passion for computing on the go. By the late 1990s, mobile computing was synonymous with portability, interactivity, user specificity, and most significant to the evolution of computing in the twenty-first century, connectivity. Hardware advances – such as metal-oxide-silicon transistors, mobile transceivers, base stations, routers, telecommunications circuits, and radio transceivers – provided the physical infrastructure for 2G, 3G, and 4G wireless networks.

Wireless communication facilitated a third revolution in computing, elevating it to an entirely new level in our lives. Early cell phones were used primarily for making phone calls and possibly sending short text messages. Within a few years, however, new communication protocols enabled us to send and receive images and videos along with voice and texts from our handheld devices. By 2010, the incredible computation and communication capabilities of mobile technologies allowed us to take such actions as exchanging money on Venmo and buying and selling stocks in real time. As of 2022, nearly 84% of the world's population used smartphones, mostly for activities other than voice conversations.

ML Emerges from a Slump

ML, which slumped for decades, bounced back in a big way in the 1990s, thanks to the availability of vastly more data and increased computational power. That marriage of big data with advanced computation set the stage for a series of ML breakthroughs. Many research communities began conceiving ways to incorporate autonomous learning into their modeling approaches. Control researchers, for instance, led a large initiative in "robust learning" for use in the design of safety-critical systems. The optimization community shifted its attention to creating new techniques for non-convex, very high-dimensional optimization problems that emerged from training DNNs. The statistical community continued its efforts in assessing and calibrating the models that were emerging from such optimization techniques.

In the realm of complex decision-making, NNs re-emerged in the form of neuro-dynamic programming. The 1996 book *Neuro-Dynamic Programming* by fellow MIT professors and colleagues

Dimitri Bertsekas and John Tsitsiklis played a pivotal role in the field's development, as did *Reinforcement Learning: An Introduction* by Richard S. Sutton and Andrew G. Barto. Research in this area focuses on deriving optimal decision strategies through an iterative process of enhancing existing decision strategies, generally referred to as RL. The work builds on the well-developed theory of optimal control and dynamic programming that traces its roots back to the 1950s and 1960s and constitutes a merger between optimal control and NNs.

Progress in decision theory made world headlines in 1997 when IBM's Deep Blue defeated world chess champion Gary Kasparov in a six-game match. It was the first victory by a computer over a reigning champ under tournament conditions, and it fulfilled the long-standing prediction that computers could outperform human experts in complex decision-making tasks. Deep Blue's key innovation was to develop a score for each configuration of the board that measured the likelihood of winning the game. Using that score, Deep Blue would calculate six to eight moves deep for both players before picking its next move. To increase the speed of Deep Blue's decision-making process, its developers trained Deep Blue on thousands of historical matches – an algorithmic technique that led to further breakthroughs in RL methods as well as twenty-first-century developments in decision-making.

By the third decade of the new millennium, developers have seamlessly integrated ML into algorithmic intelligence and solidified its position as a subset of the broader field of AI – vaguely defined as any system that may mimic or imitate human intelligence. Although one could make a philosophical argument that the boundary between ML and AI is blurred, or even irrelevant, many still distinguish between the traditional approach of predicate logic (i.e., expert systems) and the modern data-driven decision-making methods employed in ML. My view is that AI has evolved far beyond the bounds of those approaches and now encompasses a wide array of algorithmic decision-making capabilities present in a multitude of technologies and applications that may or may not imitate human intelligence (e.g., an AI system that responds to voice commands in an elevator is hardly an approximation of human intelligence).

AI's expansive capabilities now encompass a broad spectrum of applications that include natural language processing, computer vision, robotics, as well as creative tasks such as generating visual art and musical compositions. Those advances, coupled with the availability of almost incomprehensible amounts of data, have paved the way for AI systems to make informed and increasingly complex choices without explicit human intervention. AI's ever-growing ability to analyze vast data sets, identify patterns, and initiate actions is leading to a future in which automated decision-making is an integral part of our social, economic, and technological landscapes. Formally, AI systems are defined as systems that mimic human intelligence both in learning about their environment and in their capabilities to make decisions. In general conversation, AI systems broadly refer to all algorithmic methods for learning and decisions. I will contend that many systems we refer to as AI systems today are not intelligent at all.

The Rise of Embedded Systems: Fourth Revolution

As someone working to understand how we can best navigate these turbulent waters, I find societies' comfort with and dependence on distributed and mobile systems simultaneously thrilling and terrifying. To appreciate how we've arrived at this uncertain frontier, it helps to look briefly at the confluence of three additional phenomena that pro-liferated during the first two decades of the new millennium – embedded (mobile) devices, faster computers, and the capacity to implement deci-sion systems in distributed environments.

Embedded systems comprise elements of computational hard-ware (processors and memory), one or more peripheral input/output components (joystick, camera, LED display, touch screen, etc.), and specialized software programs all housed in larger devices that may include additional electronic, electrical, and mechanical parts. The list of device types that contain embedded systems is practically infinite, ranging from digital watches, dishwashers, and MP3 players to hybrid cars, medical imaging equipment, and flight control systems exemplify-ing the convergence of sensing, communication, and control. A typical Tesla electric vehicle (EV), for example, rolls off the assembly line with numerous embedded systems (spatial sensors, autopilot controls, multi-media display, etc.) as well as a nested hierarchy of embedded systems (e.g., sensors embedded in the autopilot, autopilot embedded in the vehicle).

It may be only a slight exaggeration to say that you would find it harder to avoid interacting with embedded systems in your daily routine than it would be to catch a ride into Earth's orbit on a private spacecraft. The triumph of embedded systems is also of great economic consequence. In 2009, software engineer and embedded system expert Michael Barr estimated that 98% of all new CPUs produced were being embedded. Writing on *statista.com* in February 2022, electrical and computer engineer Thomas Alsop reported the value of the global embedded market to be approximately $34.63 billion, an amount forecast to nearly double by 2027.

So Much Data, So Many Decisions

In the English language, we call a group of hummingbirds a charm. Eagles are a convocation. And geese in flight are a skein ("gaggle" is reserved for those same geese when on the ground). But what should we call a formation of unmanned aerial vehicles (UAVs)? Given that the tech community has yet to brand the UAV grouping phenomenon for marketing purposes, I'll stick to the boring descriptive phrase computer scientists and control theorists commonly use – a networked decision system.

Although such systems are the fruition of hundreds of advances across many decades, they could not exist without the convergence of sensing, communication, and decision systems made possible by faster processors, smaller computers, and embedded device hardware and software solutions. UAV formations are a great illustration of these developments. As my coauthor Michael Rinehart and I explain in our 2011 book chapter "Networked Decisions Systems" from *The Impact of Control Technology*:

> Each UAV has a local controller to control its flight, but it must also follow commanded trajectories while avoiding collisions and the like. This may require information from other nearby UAVs, ground bases, or other information sources. In addition, a leader UAV may need to provide trajectory or waypoint commands to the formation. These decisions can be communicated through the formation itself (as a multihop routing network) or through other nodes. Other examples of networked decision systems include distributed emergency response systems, interconnected transportation, energy systems, and even social networks.

We typically imagine UAVs in the order of 10s of vehicles. But the autonomous car revolution will create dynamically changing networks of hundreds of vehicles. More so, distributed and networked decision systems aren't limited solely to drones. A 2019 report for *HP®TechTakes* by Tom Gerencer noted that our daily data flow was being fed that year by approximately 20 billion devices and more than 50 billion sensors, quantities that undoubtedly have grown since the publication of this book. Just as surely, our ability to stay abreast and make sense of all that data is in catchup mode. What that means for the future of computing, and its impact on societies around the world, brings us to one of the key themes of this book – how the convergence of computation, communication, and decision systems provides the foundation for what is often called, for lack of a better, widely adopted label, AI.

Vignette

Is AI more surprising than useful? The three-game 2017 Go match pitting reigning #1 human player Ke Jie against the computer program AlphaGo Master resulted in a 3-0 victory for AlphaGo – and sparked greater worldwide fascination with AI. Developed by DeepMind, a Google subsidiary, AlphaGo's competitive success in Go, chess, and other games was the result of a combination of clever searches, a pre-learned neural network for move outcomes based on board configurations, and a vast number of self-playing trajectories. Those trajectories represented a computational innovation that incorporated strategies not typically found in human players' repertoire and gave the AI system a competitive advantage over human champions.

The Rise of Generative AI

In 2022, ChatGPT emerged as the first widely available large language model (LLM) and launched a transformative wave across the AI landscape. Armed with the ability to engage in human-like conversations and extensively trained on vast data sets, ChatGPT's debut ushered in a plethora of potential AI applications. In addition to sparking pioneering research and entrepreneurial ventures, ChatGPT's proliferation has raised concerns about the existential risks posed by AI.

Historian Yuval Harari and numerous others have joined hundreds of top AI academicians and researchers in identifying ChatGPT as a substantial existential threat to humanity. Human society, the argument goes, fundamentally relies on language-based communication. The capacity of ChatGPT and similar platforms to craft coherent and relevant narratives that influence the historical context and reshape our comprehension of human existence is highly disruptive and potentially destructive to productive interactions.

One particularly problematic LLM characteristic is hallucination – a phenomenon in which an LLM fabricates an entire narrative. Instances of hallucination arise because LLMs lack an intrinsic understanding of confidence levels and margins of error. And although LLMs can declare instances when they are uncertain, they struggle to genuinely abstain from generating content beyond their capabilities.

LLMs are just one manifestation of generative AI – a specialized field that focuses on producing output that resembles real content (be it human-created or machine-generated). Another is diffusion modeling, which uses a single image such as a dog to generate numerous additional images of dogs. Diffusion models – which use system theory and dynamics to control the stability of diffusion – offer a potent means of generating substantial volumes of labeled data from relatively small data sets. Related techniques that employ low-dimensional structures are also capable of generating much data from a relatively sparse starting point. Inaccuracy problems notwithstanding, one of the substantial benefits emerging from these technologies is the transfer learning that occurs when generative AI borrows knowledge from one field and applies it to another.

What Real Problems Are We Solving?

Given the widespread recreational applications of AI-powered LLMs, it's reasonable to ask whether AI has genuinely resolved any tangible real-world challenges. One meaningful use case can be found in autonomous control systems such as airplane autopilots, which consistently manage successful landings and enhance commercial airline safety and dependability. Although such systems haven't been labeled as AI historically, they certainly fit within our current understanding of the category. That decades-long track record of success notwithstanding, the application of the technology remains relatively circumscribed.

We have not reached the point where we trust AI to totally control the aircraft autonomously.

Applying the commercial airline scenario to a broader context exemplifies embedded systems that enable shared decision-making between humans and machines. The intricate interplay of the two entities is relevant to numerous emerging use cases. The future of passenger road vehicles, for example, is likely to include a transition from total human control to mixed autonomy (shared human-AI control) to fully autonomous AI control. When – or if – we completely cede control to machines, how do we ensure that those machines adhere to predetermined moral and ethical boundaries? We also must reiterate our initial question: what real problems does this solve, and are the risks worth the gains?

The Crucial Challenge of Protein Folding

Each cell in a human body contains between 20,000 and 100,000 distinct proteins, and each protein has its particular function within a given cell. Every protein sequence exhibits a folding behavior that enables it to perform its specific function. When that folding goes awry, biological processes essential to human health can break down, which is why researchers have been working for decades to build a better understanding of the way in which proteins fold – or fail to fold – properly.

Despite the challenge of observing that molecular process without disrupting it, scientists have been able to describe approximately 150,000 distinct protein folding patterns since the 1990s. Unfortunately, millions more such patterns remain undiscovered, potentially hampering the development of more effective therapies for devastating conditions such as cancer, cystic fibrosis, and Alzheimer's disease. Enter AlphaFold – a groundbreaking AI system developed to predict the folded 3D structure of proteins based on amino acid sequences. The underlying theory for this approach was pioneered by the 1972 recipients of the Nobel Prize in Chemistry, Christian Anfinsen, Stanford Moore, and William Howard Stein, who postulated that a protein's amino acid sequence should fully determine its structure and consequently affect its functionality.

Between 2021 and 2023, AlphaFold's owner, DeepMind, partnered with the European Bioinformatics Institute to populate a

public database (the AlphaFold Protein Structure Database) with predictions for more than 200 million protein structures. The accuracy
rates of those predictions – which may help to unlock revolutionary
treatment options for complex syndromes and new vaccines – often
match those of experimentally derived measurements. A great strength
of systems such as AlphaFold is the AI–ML self-training system that
uses an iterative loop to create an initial model, predict new folds,
evaluate them against hidden experimental folds, and then integrate
the best outcomes back into the data pool. As the reliability of various
predictions is determined, confidence levels are recorded and used to
enrich the existing database. Logic-based systems have been used to
model the interactions between protein structures, but those tend to be
approximate and static. AI–ML systems, in contrast, learn from successes and failures and improve themselves over time.

The Quest for Speed

Computer scientists, hardware and software engineers, and tech
entrepreneurs have always had their feet on the accelerator – the faster
we can compute, the better. And although our fantasies about what we
might do with more powerful machines mostly outpaced our technical
advances, the industry achieved phenomenal leaps forward in the
1990s. We witnessed a greater than tenfold increase in processor clock
speeds during that decade, and feverous competition among chip
makers such as AMD and Intel resulted in new microprocessor technologies that were smaller, cheaper, faster, and more energy efficient.

In the early 2000s, when the processing speed revolution hit a
wall related to the practical limitations of heat dissipation, the demand
for fast computing roared ahead unabated. Billions of users worldwide
became accustomed to multitasking on numerous devices and platforms
via high-speed internet connections. To satisfy this demand, engineers
devised a path around the heat dissipation barrier by creating power-
efficient processors with multiple cores, each able to solve some portion
of a larger problem simultaneously rather than sequentially.

That approach, referred to as parallel computing, historically
had been limited to activities such as scientific computing and simulations of natural and engineered systems. Researchers and industry
experts have been using parallel computing to analyze data from complex systems such as weather, navigation, traffic, finance, industrial and

agricultural production, climate, and healthcare for decades. With advances in manufacturing and programming, however, parallel computing became as much the norm for the average desktop, laptop, and smartphone as for NASA's space shuttle computer system. Today's graphics processing units (GPUs) – the next generation of processing units after CPUs – accelerate complex algorithms and AI solutions by efficiently performing parallel computations.

Omnipresent and Omnivorous Computing

At the turn of the new millennium, few of us anticipated how the platforms that would take the world by storm – Google (1996), Facebook (2004), YouTube (2005), and Twitter (2006) – would unleash a tidal wave of data and personal interactions in which we have the potential to rise or drown. Video conferencing, online multiplayer games, social media platforms, WiFi networks, the Internet, and just about everything else people around the world commonly associate with computing in 2023 are part of a distributed system. Less understood as distributed computing by the general public, but equally vital to contemporary life, are cellular networks, aircraft controls, banking systems, weather-forecasting models, windmills, and travel reservation platforms.

These examples just scratch the surface of our networked planet, such that it is difficult to imagine how contemporary global society could function without this level of interconnectivity and interchange. AI will enter each and every one of these disciplines and potentially transform them. The tools and methodologies affecting those transformations most likely will be owned and developed by domain experts – not data or computer scientists. The development of domain experts who possess the necessary data-science capabilities was the prime motivation for the creation of IDSS.

"Prediction Is Difficult, Especially If It Is about the Future." (Niels Bohr)

In the current era of data science and AI research and development, I'm mindful of the witty warning from Niels Bohr, Nobel laureate in physics, about the difficulty of making predictions based on past data and experience. On our current trajectory, however, I feel safe in projecting that digital platforms such as Facebook and Netflix will continue to gather ever greater quantities of personal data. Increasingly powerful algorithmic systems will leverage that data to provide personalized experiences and manage the behaviors of such platforms. AI systems will make more and more critical decisions related to data sharing and personalized recommendations. Even in the realm of finance, AI-powered systems will increasingly influence major investment decisions.

One possible approach to that very probable future involves pushing the capabilities of AI to the limits of our current computational power as we develop ever more sophisticated algorithms. This scenario assumes that Moore's Law – implying an exponential growth in computing resources – also will kick in and provide us with more powerful computing resources. A fundamental flaw in that approach is that it assumes that advancing hardware and software technologies guarantees progress on a multitude of challenges facing humanity.

Complications with that approach, however, are already emerging. The global climate crisis, for example, demands that we question the massive energy consumption associated with projected algorithmic and hardware advances. Speed and energy limitations may temper the adverse effects of the generative AI revolution, but we also must vigorously evaluate the knowledge being assimilated by our machines and examine the reliability of the decisions they make. We need a multifaceted, transdisciplinary approach that continually interrogates the relentless growth of AI and its potential ramifications for society.

The Arab Spring: Case in Point

Arguably, the most important societal element dictatorships control is information. Authoritarian leaders broadcast official positions on state-controlled media outlets and infiltrate the masses with spies to discourage the free expression of dissent. Information and communication technologies (ICT), particularly encrypted ones, can be used to challenge that suppression and provide a means for people to share stories, coordinate activities, and elicit help from external players. Dictatorial regimes respond by blocking such communications or smearing them with disinformation to such an extent that people lose confidence in the sources. Those methods are effective – but not foolproof.

In 2010, a YouTube video of street vendor Mohamed Bouazizi self-immolating in the city traffic of Sidi Bouzid, Tunisia, focused the world's attention on the state of poor people in that country. Information related to that event spread like wildfire throughout Tunisia and then to neighboring countries – Libya, Egypt, Syria, Yemen, and Bahrain – and set in motion the wave of uprisings known collectively as the Arab Spring. While it is unclear whether people's lives improved in any of these countries as a result of the protest, analysts and observers generally agree that ICT contributed to the social contagion that spread the unrest.

Certain and Uncertain Effects of Social Media

Many revolutions have occurred without the help of ICT, and the causal effect of ICT on various manifestations of the Arab Spring must be rigorously examined. The 2011 revolution in Egypt, however, was unquestionably the result of efforts coordinated on Facebook. A page established by Egyptian-born computer science student Wael Ghonim is credited with drawing hundreds of thousands of protesters to Cairo's Tahrir Square and launching the popular movement that brought down the country's government. Ghonim's impetus was the killing of protester Khalid Said, about whom Ghonim wrote, "Today they killed Khaled. If I don't act for his sake, tomorrow they will kill me." Ghonim's Facebook page, "Kullena Khaled Said" (We Are All Khaled Said), attracted more than a quarter of a million members within a few months.

One fascinating aspect of the Egyptian story is that Ghonim, with no formal training in activism, managed to create a highly effective forum for democratic discourse on Facebook. Rather than using the platform to propagate his own opinions, he created a forum where people could exchange ideas, consult with one another on how to advertise the cause, and ultimately coordinate actions that would disrupt the existing regime – including the physical rallies in Tahrir Square that forced the resignation of President Hosni Mubarak.

A Data-and-Society Reckoning

I must stress that while Facebook in Egypt had a causal effect on the uprising in Tahrir Square, we cannot assert the counterfactual causality that if Facebook did not exist, the uprising would not have happened. We need more research into other causal forces to make such an assertion. As for the broader connection between social media usage and democratic activism, Non-resident senior fellow Sahar Khamis provided an interesting analysis for Arab Center Washington DC. In her 2020 article "Media Use and Its Anomalies a Decade after the Arab Spring," Khamis observed that increases in social media use did not result in increased activism in repressed countries. Rather, it appears to have shifted such activism to the diaspora of individuals who fled to countries where they could speak freely. Khamis's observations indicate that many years after the revolution, oppressive regimes may have found other ways of exerting control over their citizens.

From the cascade of events associated with the Arab Spring to election interference in Ukraine in 2014 and the US in 2016, we now know that massive amounts of data and social networking may be weaponized to foment misunderstanding and chaos as readily as they can be directed toward social and technical progress. Distributed computing architecture, combined with the proliferation of wireless and mobile network solutions in the 1990s, paved the way for a data deluge and social media revolution that rocked our world in the two decades that followed – and triggered a digital reckoning that only just came into focus in the 2020s.

When AI Undercuts Democratic Principles and Practices

A prime example of the looming digital reckoning can be found in the Cambridge Analytica-Facebook scandal, a complex situation associated with the 2016 US presidential election in which Facebook was implicated in the sale of millions of data sets belonging to its individual subscribers. The incident highlighted ethical concerns surrounding the misuse of user data as well as the broader implications for democracy and the need to regulate the use of such data in political campaigns. It also illustrated the delicate balance between the role social media platforms play in facilitating communication and the responsibility those platforms must bear to protect the privacy and integrity of individuals and elections.

In general terms, the scandal involved the extraction of intricate psychological profiles by Cambridge Analytica from Facebook user data. That information was used to gain insights into the personalities and preferences of individual Facebook users. Those psychological profiles were subsequently leveraged to target individuals with pinpoint political advertising. If a person was judged to be anxious, for example, that person might be shown advertising on their Facebook page related to a terrorist act, with the goal being to sway that person's political views or biases toward a specific candidate or policy.

More Questions than Answers

The Cambridge Analytica-Facebook scandal raised numerous urgent ethical questions about ML and AI that we're only just beginning to grapple with. Can those technologies, for instance, genuinely predict the emotional responses of individuals to particular information? Although it is correct to say that the interdisciplinary field of AI combines machines, behavior analysis, neuroscience, and psychology, many researchers dispute whether we have reached the point where such predictions are entirely accurate. Intertwined with that technical question is the critical ethical concern that Facebook violated the privacy of users when it communicated and shared sensitive personal data without obtaining explicit consent.

Assessing the causal influence and culpability of Cambridge Analytica's tactics related to the outcome of the election remains extremely challenging. Voting behavior often is private and difficult to monitor, and some experts contend that people typically stick to their political convictions regardless of being psychologically targeted by advertising. For its part, Cambridge Analytica asserted that they did not run such ads themselves but simply provided the data to the Trump campaign. That line of argument raises the specter of voter data manipulation by campaign operatives. Should we, as a democratic society, put regulations in place that restrict the extent to which such data can be utilized to influence voters? Building on questions of the manipulation of individual voters, we must interrogate network effects and consensus. Manipulating information and individuals within social networks can lead to different outcomes that are difficult to predict and control. Should we allow AI tools to be used without regulation, given the extent to which those tools can be abused to skew public understanding and consensus?

3 WHO – AND WHAT – SHOULD DRIVE DECISION-MAKING?
Harnessing Data for the Good of Society

In late 2023, the *New York Times* filed a copyright-infringement lawsuit in US federal court alleging that ChatGPT creators OpenAI and Microsoft used *NYT's* material without permission to train its chatbots. Earlier that same year, the European Union enacted the world's first international regulatory framework for AI. And in 2018, researchers at Harvard and MIT launched a collaboration with the Privacy and Data Protection Directorate of the Canadian government to examine the human-rights ramifications of AI.

The consequences of those and similar efforts to reign in mostly unfettered use of data for profit and power will likely take decades to unfold. The deliberative nature of that process makes it all the more important that as many private individuals, academicians, public servants, advocacy groups, and corporate decision-makers as possible join the debate. In this chapter, we hope to help lay the foundation for some of those conversations by introducing a few key topics and questions. How do we strike the right balance between mathematical logic and social justice? Can we program out the persistent biases that have plagued civilization for millennia? How much control – and accountability – should humans retain over generative systems? Should we apply the same set of ethics to machines as we currently do to humans? Must we simply accept that money makes the world go 'round and hope that the free market will deliver what's best for society in the long run?

Early Examples of Promises and Pitfalls

AI-informed chemical experiments produce revolutionary new materials over a period of months rather than years. ML algorithms discover previously unknown craters on the surface of Mars. AI-guided lab robots unlock promising clean-energy solutions 1,000 times faster than conventional laboratory approaches. Continuously learning algorithms study pedestrian behaviors to make self-driving cars safer at intersections.

The flipside of such revolutionary advances is the dystopian horrors. Chatbots spew racist rhetoric and generate inflammatory emails. Cameras surveil Beijing pedestrians to spot "criminal" gaits. Autonomous vehicles strike and kill pedestrians. Algorithms use proxies to race to assess loan applications. These real-life nightmares loom large in our collective imagination and inspire the general public's distrust of the data-driven computation-based and computation-aided decision-making commonly referred to as AI and ML.

Algorithmic Logic versus Justice

From groundbreaking drugs and healthcare strategies to clean energy networks and sustainable urban development, the potential of AI and ML to help us solve our most vexing and life-threatening problems is irrefutable. The challenge lies in remaining clear-eyed and critical about what our technological wonders do and do not do well. Just because we can program such tools to be logically consistent does not make them rational or socially beneficial.

We also must question the limits of our reason in leading us to fair and equitable decision systems. When our controlling biases – whether conscious or unconscious – reinforce the status quo, existing regimens of oppression and inequity will persist. Data are susceptible to willful misuse and misinterpretation for narrow, anti-social objectives, and individuals are all too easily inspired to engage in computationally amplified behaviors that sow confusion, distrust, and division. Few of us working in computation-related fields in the late twentieth and early twenty-first centuries anticipated how rapidly AI and ML technologies could be weaponized and deployed for such purposes.

If recent human history has taught us anything, it's that we are not predominantly rational beings. The irrational aspects of our natures often generate compelling arguments for unjust and inhumane actions and institutional practices. Whatever we create with AI, ML, and the new technologies that follow in those wakes, we must never allow ourselves to be transformed from thinkers and doers into followers and facilitators.

Humans versus Distributed Computing: An AI Showdown?

Like it or not, decisions that directly influence individual lives, shape societies, and affect the health of our planet will continue to be guided by data that is collected, analyzed, reported, and, in some cases, acted on by distributed agents (e.g., physical electronic sensors, data sharing bots, problem-solving, and implementation algorithms) with AI and ML capabilities. What we gain and what we lose as a consequence will depend on the nature and depth of our engagement with the distributed decision systems we've created. The technologies of data gathering, computation, and data-driven decisions are racing ahead, and we must accelerate our own mastery of these new capabilities to reap the societal benefits they promise. Alarmists caution that we are about to, or already have, cross the Rubicon into an us-versus-them relationship with the distributed agents we've created by voluntarily surrendering too much power to them. Much about the future of AI and ML is up for grabs, but one thing is clear – machines certainly will be smarter than humans if we persist in acting dumber than machines. As mathematician Norbert Wiener expressed it, "The world of the future will be an even more demanding struggle against the limitations of our intelligence, not a comfortable hammock in which we can lie down to be waited upon by our robot slaves."

A simple example of a distributed-agent system is local traffic-camera enforcement. Violating posted speed restrictions triggers a photograph or two of your vehicle and license plate and a potential monetary penalty. The majority of us accept our mistake, pay the fine, and think no more of it. In doing so, we fail to appreciate the full set of automated capabilities that measure and record our behavior, analyze it in relation to existing laws, and report it to other components within the system – a system that has the authority to issue us a ticket and create a permanent record of our moving violations without any direct human intervention.

The Persistent Challenges of Bias

Traffic-camera enforcement may seem relatively innocuous until you apply the principles and components of such systems to more complex law enforcement activities. We know that predictive policing tools, for example, are imbued with racial biases when algorithms are trained on pre-existing arrest data from police departments. For decades, police have made more arrests in neighborhoods with higher percentages of Black and Brown residents. The use of such data teaches AI tools to steer more law enforcement to those areas, resulting in still more arrests – thus perpetuating a vicious data-driven cycle of racist policing.

Facial recognition tools have the alarming potential to perpetuate their own biases. Professor Craig Watkins, an MLK fellow at MIT and IDSS, recounts a distressing incident involving a young Black man who, in the presence of his family and friends, was arrested under suspicion of shoplifting expensive watches worth more than $4,000. Subsequent thorough investigations revealed that the police had apprehended the wrong individual. In light of that and similar instances, builders and users of these technologies must carefully examine what led to such grave mistakes.

Numerous researchers have documented that facial recognition algorithms exhibit significant errors when applied to individuals with darker skin tones. Their work demonstrates that the problems stem entirely from the practice of training these algorithms on biased data (predominantly White). In the specific case highlighted by Watkins, the facial recognition algorithm mistakenly identified the wrong person as a result of its flawed understanding of diverse facial features and appearances. The consequences of such errors can be severe, leading to innocent individuals being wrongly accused and negatively impacted by unintentionally biased technologies.

Alternative Training Presents Its Own Problems

Unfortunately, efforts to "train out" those biases have shown that technical fixes are easier to imagine than to implement. As reported in *MIT Technology Review* in January 2021, Carnegie Mellon researchers Nil-Jana Akpinar and Alexandra Chouldechova demonstrated that training predictive policing algorithms in ways purported to lessen bias had very little actual benefit.

When the team focused their "well-trained" tool on Bogotá, Colombia, they discovered that the AI algorithm underreported actual hotspots by roughly 80% in areas with few victim reports of crime and overreported by 20% in areas with a larger number of reports. Despite such fundamental flaws in predictive-policing AI, private surveillance companies are racing ahead with complex networks of drones, security cameras, smartphone trackers, and license plate readers (i.e., distributed agents) that produce compelling AI-driven data fusions that have law-enforcement agencies chomping at the bit. But are we at risk of becoming enamored of and dependent on these elaborate systems before we know if they are just and equitable?

The Bogotá study shows how self-fulfilling phenomena – in this case, more arrest data from a particular geography suggests increased surveillance, which leads to more arrests – can unintentionally weaponize data against the communities it could be helping. Negative bias also can infect the use of data when human programmers lack the domain expertise to account for all the appropriate independent variables within a domain-specific decision-making system.

These overlooked variables, or confounding factors, result in over-simplified models and inherently biased decisions. Preventable, but sadly prevalent, examples of such bias occur in loan approval algorithms. When such a system is supplied with data showing that Black and Brown borrowers historically have higher rates of mortgage defaults than the general population, individual customers from those groups are more likely to be denied loans and refused opportunities to appeal the determinations. Consequently, this becomes a barrier to building wealth among such communities and reinforces a vicious cycle.

Although those rejections may appear justified to a software engineer focused on a single metric, economists and sociologists tell us that historical inequities in incomes, job stability, career opportunities, access to education, and family circumstances – that is, confounding factors – should be considered. In short, you must be more than a skilled programmer or computer scientist to create AI and ML tools that use data equitably and promote the greater good of society. Understanding the importance of sampling bias, data imbalance, confounders, and causality in inference and learning is key, and I'll talk a bit more about that in the next chapter.

Ethical Decision-Making

Ethics provide societies with systems of acceptable behavior, but those guidelines are not immutable. A society may change what it collectively considers acceptable through changes in law or the evolution of social norms. Humans have lived with that phenomenon for generations, but researchers are only just beginning to grapple with the implications of malleable ethics for AI technologies.

In the 2015 *MIT Technology Review* article "Why Self-Driving Cars Must Be Programmed to Kill," cognitive psychologist Jean-François Bonnefon discusses research he and colleagues conducted on the ethical complexities surrounding autonomous vehicles. The work examined a very probable scenario that poses a complex moral dilemma – should a self-driving car prioritize the safety of its passengers or the lives of pedestrians outside the vehicle?

The question is complicated by an intricate interplay of ethics and economics, and the potential ramifications for consumers and manufacturers are immense. One approach is to consistently prioritize the lives of pedestrians, which presents a commercial downside of potentially putting drivers (aka buyers) of autonomous vehicles at greater risk. An alternative to that scenario is to equip cars with the ability to assess casualty numbers and make decisions that minimize the overall death toll per incident – a utilitarian model that seems distant from our human decision-making processes.

The conundrum grows when you consider two contradictory projections for the technology – while autonomous systems have the potential to significantly reduce the overall number of accidents, they also may lead to a higher aggregate death toll for drivers or pedestrians. Who will decide where the correct balance lies between individual safety and collective wellbeing? Bonnefon's research on this question examined the role of public opinion in determining the right course of action. He and his colleagues discovered an overall preference for the utilitarian approach of minimizing casualties. They also discovered a paradox. People say they prefer the concept of self-driving cars that sacrifice the occupants to protect people outside the vehicle – as long as they don't have to drive such a vehicle themselves. That finding underscores the complexity of applying utilitarian principles to AI technologies.

One Standard for Machines, Another for Humans?

Curiously, we don't train human drivers to calculate potential casualties when navigating complex situations. But why isn't casualty assessment part of driver education? And what accounts for our greater comfort with the imperfect outcomes of human decisions, even if those decisions result in higher casualty rates? People generally seem to be more willing to forgive human operators for car accidents than their autonomous counterparts.

Our near-zero tolerance for errors by AI systems appears to vary, however, depending on the application. While we expect autonomous vehicles to perform flawlessly, we accept a wider range of errors in decisions involving loan approvals or text generated by LLMs. The ethical framework suggested by this dual bifurcated mindset warrants examination. Does ethical education play a role in fostering responsible behavior? Could it have deterred the creation and use of the atomic bomb, a devastating weapon that claimed the lives of 150,000 people in a single detonation? Are we on track to introduce similarly destructive inventions into the world because we fail to interrogate the intricate relationship among ethics, decision-making, and the technologies we create and deploy.

Sadly, the pace of technological advancement is outpacing our capacity to fully grasp the societal and humanistic consequences of deployment. We must discipline ourselves to consistently consider the social and ethical ramifications of potent technologies such as AI and ML, and we must learn from our past. A prior generation argued fervently that certain television content could be harmful to young children. Although the outcomes were mixed, those debates underscored the significance of regulating televised content based on age appropriateness.

In our day, the analogous debate seems to have fizzled. We've largely surrendered to the widespread availability of the internet, allowing very young children to access highly potent material they are ill-equipped to comprehend. I contend, however, that we must not use ease of access as an excuse to disregard the responsibilities we bear toward society. Perhaps a robust debate could generate fundamental guiding principles for the future of AI applications.

The Challenge Is Larger for Large Language Models (LLMs)

The concept of robustness in ML highlights the surprising vulnerability of these algorithms to the smallest intentional alterations. The introduction of minor, purposeful changes to objects can yield entirely new outcomes – a phenomenon covered nicely in the 2013 paper "Intriguing properties of neural networks" by Christian Szegedy and colleagues. A slight perturbation to a stop sign, for example, can cause a computer vision algorithm to perceive it as a speed-limit sign. A minor adjustment to specific pixels in an image can transform a panda into the semblance of a gibbon, even when the adjustments are imperceptible to the human eye. Can we understand the inner workings of our machines well enough to track the details they identify and subsequently amplify?

That perturbation phenomenon extends beyond individual occurrences and raises broad concerns. Unstructured ML systems are susceptible to learning entirely incorrect associations that potentially lead them to highlight strange and unrelated attributes within images. The phenomenon raises crucial questions about how to ensure the robustness, learnability, and confidence of these algorithms. To address the challenge, we must revisit the fundamental principles of ML, use accurate and relevant data, select appropriate models, employ suitable algorithms, and provide robust statistical guarantees. Unfortunately, the lack of robustness in ML extends to LLMs. These models lack a conscious understanding of when they provide coherent information versus when they assemble ideas at random. As with other computer vision algorithms, LLMs must harness the power of statistical accuracy to ensure the reliability of the information they generate.

Back to Causality

Causality, in my opinion, remains the Holy Grail in the pursuit of algorithmic fairness. We cannot conduct randomized trials of police brutality, so we must join forces with sociologists and law-enforcement professionals to precisely understand all contributing factors. In the case of excessive force by a White officer against a Black civilian, we must account for individual prejudice, law-enforcement hiring and training protocols, previous encounters with police, and high-crime-neighborhood designations, among other factors. I am encouraged by the enthusiasm of many of my colleagues at IDSS for such lines of research.

To grasp the essence of causal analysis in connection with police brutality, we can examine the controversial stop-and-frisk policy implemented in New York City that was credited by some in law enforcement with reducing crime rates. It has been widely argued, however, that the policy led to discrimination – specifically, a disproportionate number of stop-and-frisk incidents conducted on Black and Hispanic individuals. To validate this claim, we need to develop a model to understand how such stop-and-frisk events may arise. We can, for example, construct an influence diagram in which a frisk is caused by race (an observable element), by an officer's suspicion that an individual is carrying a weapon a (nonobservable element), or by some combination of the two. The outcome of the suspicion is observed when a frisk is conducted – revealing whether or not the individual is in possession of a weapon. The challenge lies in the fact that a police officer can only suspect if someone might be carrying a weapon but cannot observe the outcome until they perform the frisk. What the officer can observe before the frisk, of course, is the race of the individual being stopped.

When we gather data on stop-and-frisk incidents, we can construct an influence diagram that estimates the effects of race and suspicion on the likelihood of being frisked. That also allows us to explore counterfactual questions such as whether an individual would have been stopped if they were White. Researchers, including Matt Kusner and his colleagues in their 2017 article "Counterfactual Fairness," have presented compelling evidence of bias in stop-and-frisk arrests. They suggest that race played a significant role in the decision-making process, leading to a disproportionate number of frisks on Black and Hispanic individuals – even when suspicion of carrying a weapon was controlled for. We must recognize, however, that causal analysis requires deep expertise and great care. An influence diagram may be inconclusive or incorrect if it omits one or more key variables (e.g., location) that may have influenced outcomes. This careful analysis was exercised in the paper by Kusner referenced earlier.

As a standard of practice, researchers routinely examine a variety of potential confounders to conclude causality. In "A large-scale analysis of racial disparities in police stops across the United States," for example, Emma Pierson and 10 colleagues conducted a comprehensive examination of racial disparities in police stops. By analyzing a data set comprising nearly 100 million traffic stops conducted nationwide, the team revealed a consequential confounder – that Black drivers were less likely to be stopped after sunset. That observation is significant because it corresponds to the so-called veil of darkness (i.e., a time when a driver's race is not easily identified), which indicates the potential influence of racial bias in stop decisions. By analyzing search rates among stopped drivers and the likelihood of discovering contraband, the study also suggests that the threshold for searching Black and Hispanic drivers is lower than that for White drivers.

Who Will Drive Decisions: The Legal Landscape

Companies, countries, states, municipalities, universities, and other large entities increasingly rely on data-driven decision-making. As they develop AI systems to achieve their objectives, regulating those systems – and the use of external data feeding such systems – is an immense challenge for policymakers. Given the pervasive placement of sensors, can anyone realistically expect their personal data to be immune from harvesting and manipulation?

The fundamental legal frameworks we construct must address issues of data privacy and ownership. Those frameworks also must resolve the inherent conflicts of interest among individuals and organizations. When we use Google search, for example, Google contends that it is offering us a free service. Is it truly free? And does the absence of a monetary charge entitle Google to access and use our data? Google and other commercial entities have asserted that you should pay a fee to protect your privacy. The question is further complicated by the fact that your privacy may also be invaded when the data of your family members and friends are harvested. I'll have more to say about that later in this chapter.

The European Union (EU) has been much more systematic in creating and enforcing regulations on privacy and use of individuals' data. The EU's General Data Privacy Regulations (GDPR), for example, are designed to prevent harmful misuse of personal data by imposing substantial penalties on entities that mishandle private individual information. The GDPR undoubtedly plays a crucial role in safeguarding privacy, but economists Roslyn Mae Layton and Silvia Elaluf-Calderwood argue in their 2020 paper "A social economic analysis of the impact of GDPR on security and privacy practices" that such regulations pose challenges for small tech companies striving to develop meaningful products.

Layton and Elaluf-Calderwood contend that smaller EU enterprises are hindered when competing with US-based global giants such as Google, which face fewer restrictions than EU companies and can more easily absorb the financial impact of GDPR penalties within their substantial profit margins. That potentially unintended consequence has inspired some critics to call GDPR the "Google Data Privacy Regulation." The critiques highlight a key difficulty with region-specific regulations – they inadvertently stifle innovation in more-heavily regulated zones. Such is the intricate and interconnected nature of privacy laws in the global marketplace.

As we transition toward more automated solutions and AI becomes integral to decision-making processes, we must monitor for potential biases in systems designed to process data and make decisions. Ultimately, the responsibility to prevent bias should rest with the individuals who design these systems. Unfortunately, the discovery of systemic biases often occurs after multiple algorithmic iterations, a problem that becomes more complex when AI systems are the result of federated learning. The very nature of these technologies poses complicated legal challenges at the intersection of data use and AI regulation – for developers and enforcement bodies alike.

Vignette

Consider a healthcare AI system that provides initial diagnoses to patients, a tool that may depend upon multiple decentralized data sets and models developed in a distributed manner. The question of how we assess the compliance of such a system is critical – as is how we assign responsibility for any bias we uncover in the system. The process of debiasing in data sets and learning methods requires a thorough understanding of the system architecture that identifies the complete value chain. The lackluster response to that challenge in healthcare systems thus far stands in contrast to safety compliance in the aviation industry, where systems are built with extensive domain knowledge, models, and experience.

Differential Privacy

Even when algorithms process individual data, the critical question of whether the outcomes adequately protect data privacy persists.

In their influential 2006 paper "Calibrating Noise to Sensitivity in Private Data Analysis," researchers Cynthia Dwork, Frank McSherry, Kobbi Nissim, and Adam Smith formalized the concept of "differential privacy" within algorithms. By carefully adding calibrated noise to data so that it does not materially alter the outcome of the algorithmic process, the algorithm remains insensitive to any single data point and is deemed differentially private. This property ensures that the algorithm cannot be reverse-engineered or used to infer private information from its output.

Designing such algorithms comes with specific constraints, and not all algorithms can feasibly be made differentially private. Algorithms that calculate the median of a data set, for instance, are highly sensitive to noise and require precise data. Algorithms that compute averages, on the other hand, can be made differentially private simply by introducing noise to the sum of the data points. As of 2024, such differentially private algorithms are being considered as potential alternatives to regulatory measures and have gained significant adoption rates among researchers and industry professionals. We still have much to learn about the potential of this approach, and we must consider it in the larger context of data set externalities and a nuanced definition of one's data (as you will see later in this chapter).

Humans Must Remain Accountable

As we shift the focus of decision-making in many sectors of society, it is imperative that we not cede decision-making entirely to machines. For every application, we must assess how much authority for final decisions individuals should retain. This is especially true for intricately interconnected systems in which humans may struggle to comprehend the multifaceted consequences of their choices. Reflecting on incidents related to the Chernobyl nuclear meltdown, for example, engineers and policymakers agreed that human intervention potentially contributed to this disaster (e.g., human operators prematurely launched a catastrophic safety test that would have been correctly delayed by an automatic control system). Granting that this mistake may have been the last fatal error in a string of safety violations, we can understand that the complexity of the systems at work could have clouded human perception of the devastating consequences of a single real-time action.

Our constructed systems should serve as aids to our tasks rather than as surrogates for human decision-making. This is especially true when the job involves more than routine decisions based on a fixed set of variables. ML methods are excelling in areas such as drug design, for example, but we must maintain our understanding of the underlying biology or chemistry to make the most of the tools – especially as our understanding of these domains evolves over time. That approach will expedite the process of discovery across various fields and foster greater innovation in the application of data science and AI to complex problems.

We must also bear in mind that any technology can be applied in negative ways – ML and generative AI are no exceptions. What makes these systems distinctly dangerous, however, is their ability to invent artificial situations and contexts that seem real and that appear to be the outcome of human decision-making. This may have a profound impact on how devious such systems can be, thus adding to the challenge of monitoring and regulating such systems even as we continue to develop and deploy them.

Market Forces and Data Monetization: Case in Point

Since the first digital advertisements appeared in 1994, the worldwide online ad market has grown to approximately $400 billion. Platforms not only enable online social media and e-commerce, they also produce loops of continuous feedback in which the information gathered about users is reflected back to them in the form of product recommendations and other marketing efforts. Such recommendations directly influence people's behavior by nudging their decision-making on just about everything – from what moisturizer to try or automobile to buy to which candidates they should support in the next election.

On the simpler end of the nudging spectrum, a platform such as Netflix focuses solely on its own products. It uses past data on what users watch and how they rate movies and series to build predictive models of people's interests. The company uses collaborative filtering – a predictive model that analyzes groups of customers based on derived similarities – to translate shared behaviors into more accurate recommendations. The downside of this approach is that it tends to produce relatively narrow genre recommendations for many groupings. To counter that problem, Netflix has adopted more sophisticated algorithms that use exploration/exploitation strategies to optimize the outcomes of its recommendations. Such algorithms toggle between making recommendations that align with the customer's historical viewership profile and suggesting new movies to explore the customer's interests.

On the more complicated end of the spectrum, platforms such as Amazon and Google sell advertising opportunities to a very large set of companies that are eager to market a wide range of products. As a consequence, when you sign in to Amazon, for example, a portion of the page you see is populated with ads from companies intent on targeting you. While each of those companies may have its own historical data about you, they also have access to a market in which they can buy additional data about you and other individual users – a highly inefficient, though still lucrative, market model.

Using consumer's purchased data and existing predictive models, each company placing ads on Amazon decides how much to bid for a particular piece of screen space. The company also uses the data to determine which product to market specifically to you. If you click on the ad, the company's algorithm adds this new experimental data point to its knowledge of your interests and buying habits. Your individual click adds to the overall click rate, which is the most prevalent metric of success in digital advertising markets.

How Data Markets Can Amplify Biases

As is typical of markets, the big players in data markets have outsized power. A large company that can bid higher on available ad space holds a competitive advantage over smaller companies, which often are priced out unless they have a niche product of keen interest to a particular group of people. Such markets also can be skewed in how they reinforce misperceptions and amplify biases.

In their research paper *"Algorithmic Bias: A study of data-based discrimination in the serving of ads in Social Media,"* Anja Lambrecht and Catherine E. Tucker questioned why ads for STEM programs tend to be more heavily targeted toward men than women. The disparity is counterintuitive –women demonstrate strong interest in STEM, they are at least as likely to click on such ads as men, and colleges and universities are making concerted efforts to attract more women to their STEM programs through marketing.

It turns out that this counterproductive outcome is driven by the nature of the digital advertising marketplace. In general, retailers targeting ads to women typically bid higher for the available ad space on websites than the institutions and organizations seeking to market STEM programs. Unable to win pricey ad space targeting female consumers, STEM providers are reaching more men than women by default rather than intent. This produces a double-negative effect of attracting more men than women to STEM and creating new biased data that appears to show less interest among women. The harms are both to women and to the STEM education ecosystem.

What Are You Getting for Your Data?

The example of STEM advertising raises an interesting question about the fuel on which the digital advertising market runs. The value of the product advertisers pay for is not derived from the virtual real estate on the platform (Google, Safari, Firefox, etc.) where the ad appears but the data points advertisers collect about you when you click on their digital ad – namely, that you are interested in their product. Essentially, you are the product, although the platform is collecting all the revenue. Should you be compensated for creating value for the platform? In what sense are you the owner of this data about yourself?

Within the context of this data marketplace, you could attempt the equivalent of a work stoppage. If you and other platform users collectively refused to click on any ads, the value of the ad space would evaporate and that digital market would disappear. Theoretically, the stoppage could give you leverage to demand that the platform compensate you for your clicks. The most obvious flaw in this scenario is the highly unlikely and extremely difficult global coordination it would require among you and millions of other platform users.

Stoppage or not, platforms enable this exchange because they provide a service (e-commerce for Amazon and the search for Google). Such companies have argued that if users wanted ownership of their data, then they should pay for the service (or equivalently pay to retain their ownership). This value exchange is extremely challenging from an economic perspective as the value of data is driven from the way it is utilized – it does not have intrinsic value. Data ownership and privacy are likely to remain a challenge within these platforms and markets.

Externalities in Data Markets: What Defines Your Data

When information about individual users is being bought and sold in the marketplace, as discussed above, we must examine the question of externality –a side-effect or consequence in commercial activity that affects third parties without being reflected in the cost of the goods or services being sold. When, for example, data about you is sold to multiple companies, the value of that data is reduced for each company that purchases it. The mere fact that a competitor has the same information about you causes negative utility for other companies holding that data.

From the perspective of you as the data commodity, information about you may be gathered as a side-effect of online activity undertaken by some other user whose behavior is correlated to yours. Web-based genealogical and genetics platforms such as *23andMe* and *Ancestry* expose potential downsides for individual users. These businesses are another form of data market in which you pay a fee to learn about your lineage and ancestors and possibly learn about genetic diseases in your family tree. The resulting database of genetic information is extremely valuable and could be used against you. It doesn't take a great imaginative leap to foresee that your genetic predisposition for certain diseases could result in an outsized insurance premium one day.

The loss of privacy inherent in such scenarios, while concerning, has upsides that are welcomed by many individuals, organizations, and government entities. The 2018 arrest of a suspect in the notorious "Golden State Killer" case from the 1970s and 1980s owes much to the open-source genealogy website *GEDmatch*. Investigators were able to comb through numerous genetic profiles without a court order until they zeroed in on the genetic profile of someone who appeared to be related to the killer. By surveilling their prime suspect, investigators were able to collect a contemporary DNA sample that provided strong evidence that the suspect was the killer. A loss for privacy advocates and a win for law enforcement – and a reminder that notions of privacy cannot be assessed in isolation from externalities.

4 A TRANSDISCIPLINE IS BORN

When we launched the MIT IDSS in the summer of 2015, none of us imagined that it would be coming of age as an academic transdiscipline when a global pandemic struck. Crafting responses and measuring the impact of COVID-19 on our communities reminded us all that some phenomena are impossible to quantify. And yet, we recognized that we were confronting a profound proof-of-concept moment for our discipline – a discipline that prominently features actionable quantitative analysis in its value proposition.

At that time, my colleagues and I were aware of other researchers and academicians at institutions around the world seeking to demonstrate greater utility and relevance of emerging data-science tools and methods. While those initiatives were instructive and inspiring, we all felt we were on to something game-changing and special because our work had direct impacts on decisions that needed to be made right away.

We created IDSS specifically to address great societal challenges and to use scientific information to support sound policymaking. Probability and statistics are effective tools for addressing problems with uncertainty, and if ever there was a time to marshal our collective, transdisciplinary expertise and help decision-makers confront a crisis with timely, ethical, and equitable initiatives, this was it. It was also clear, however, that we would have to operate outside our comfort zones of conventional academic research, peer review, and publication cycles if we were to provide relevant, real-time guidance. Add to these challenges the fact that none of us had specific expertise in pandemics.

In April 2020, just weeks into the COVID-related shutdowns across the US, we created a new volunteer collaboration within IDSS called ISOLAT. The group held daily virtual meetings for months to discuss the findings of topic-driven subgroups. We committed ourselves to address three broad areas of data analysis related to the crisis: creating a data structure of heterogeneous data sets (e.g., the spread of virus, mobility, interventions); performing predictions of various critical time-dependent variables; and understanding the effects of intervention and policies on the spread of this virus. From the outset, our work addressed core issues of equity, economic and health tradeoffs, and the design of policies to mitigate the risks of infections.

I'll explain more about the specific research findings and response strategies ISOLAT produced later on. In this chapter, I set a broader context for understanding how dynamic initiatives such as ISOLAT, as well as other initiatives within IDSS broadly, came into being and how they differ from the way we've typically performed research in science and technology. To understand why things are changing in institutions around the world, we must zoom out a bit and talk more generally about disciplines – what they are, why they matter, and what they do well.

Why Disciplines Matter

Disciplines loom large as an organizing principle in global higher education. Almost every university in the world shares a substantially analogous set of degrees that students can pursue and use as launchpads to professional careers or further study – and for good reason. Disciplinary training creates enormous efficiencies in providing a reliable stream of capable young people to fill roles that we, as a developed society, have found useful and necessary. But how do we know a discipline when we see one, and why is it useful for scholars, researchers, and practitioners to align themselves with a discipline? In my experience, an academic discipline comprises five key attributes: community (e.g., conferences, symposia, academic departments); journals; educational track reduced to a core set of topics designed to instill a distinct way of thinking about the problems it attempts to solve; shared understanding of outstanding challenges, open problems, and common knowledge; and defined criteria for evaluating suitability for hiring, promotion, and tenure.

Disciplines are productive, stable, and subject to administration. Those qualities help disciplines retain institutional backing, secure space and equipment, and garner financial support. On the teaching side, a discipline provides a systematic path to reaching a defined set of educational objectives. Knowledge is passed on and expanded in a reliable progression. We can measure outcomes by students' attainment of disciplinary language, insights, and methodologies. And graduates can use the toolkits they acquire to become successful and productive members of society. They also find it relatively straightforward to land teaching roles in their disciplines at other universities when they choose that career path.

For researchers, disciplines provide stable, well-defined environments in which to question the known and the unknown, conduct experiments and gather data, advance hypotheses, and prove theories. Significantly, this research isn't required to have obvious and immediate relevance or application to our everyday lives – and that's a very good thing. Although problem-driven research is responsible for many game-changing advances, some of the most important breakthroughs in modern human history originated in the pursuit of knowledge for knowledge's sake within the framework of an academic discipline. The study of bacteria, for example, resulted in the discovery of penicillin. Early inquiries in physics, gravity, and astrophysics laid the foundation for countless modern technologies. Nuclear physics gave us an astonishing means of generating electricity and fundamental research in genomics resulting in mRNA vaccines. And the list goes on.

Challenges of the Disciplinary Model

Disciplines, as traditionally administered, do have limitations. The passionate focus on a prescribed set of tools, methods, and phenomena essential to the formation of a discipline necessarily screens out a wide swath of interesting and urgent questions – many of which are examined by other disciplines. On the whole, members of a particular discipline value the good work being done in other disciplines. Turf wars are infrequent, though not unheard of. In all honesty, I'm surprised such conflicts are as rare as they are given the high-stakes competition for status, space, and funding within most university environments.

In truth, no one field – be it sociology, computer science, economics, political science, or any other traditional discipline – is fully equipped to tackle all facets of extremely complex and rapidly evolving conundrums such as unanticipated consequences related to digital media in general and social media. When we try to work together on something that lends itself to collaboration, however, we sometimes struggle to understand one another's languages and methodologies. This was particularly evident in the early days of what may come to be known as the era of big data.

Happily, myriad societal challenges spanning various disciplines have spurred a new form of research – multidisciplinary and interdisciplinary projects. In a precise sense, these collaborations involve the merging of multiple disciplines and often entail the transfer of knowledge from one domain to another. Within IDSS, however, we assert that it is essential to surpass this approach such that the intersection of disciplines involving Data, Systems, and Society (DSS) gives rise to novel habits of mind and problem formulation. We designate this evolving realm as transdiscipline. This distinction, although not very tight, has been made to some extent by various researchers. I recommend the 2009 work of Romanian physicist Basarab Nicolescu for more background, including "Transdisciplinarity – Past, Present and Future."

Disciplinarity: Multi, Inter, and Trans

Here are three examples that highlight the key distinctions among multidisciplinary, interdisciplinary, and transdisciplinary approaches. Consider, in the first instance, research into bullying behavior on the internet. That line of inquiry comprises components from social interactions, psychology, and digital networks. Analyzing and potentially addressing this complex problem requires individuals from these diverse areas to interact and collaborate, making it an interaction among multiple disciplines (i.e., multidisciplinary).

Contemplate next the evolution of molecular biology, a field that focuses on the biochemical processes within a cell such as DNA replication. The convergence of contributions from genetics, physics, and chemistry required knowledge transfers among all three disciplines. The resulting interdisciplinary research led to breakthroughs that none of the three disciplines could have achieved in isolation. As a relatively new and distinct discipline, molecular biology continues to draw on its origins even as it significantly influences new work in biology and genetics.

In contrast to those first two examples, mathematics is a prime example of a transdisciplinary field. It empowers other disciplines to transcend conventional boundaries and facilitates journeys into new frontiers. As with other transdisciplines, mathematics embeds itself in existing fields (e.g., economics, computer science, management, etc.) and fosters a seamless transfer of knowledge across traditional boundaries. Its integration into numerous disciplines enhances the penetrability of disciplinary siloes and allows problems to be approached from new and invigorating angles. As you'll see later in this chapter, the transdisciplinarity of mathematics provided an important frame of reference when we launched the new transdiscipline of DSS.

Early Culture Clashes over Data

One difficulty my MIT colleagues and I encountered in the late 1990s was a cultural mismatch among disciplines in the collecting and processing of data. To a considerable extent, computer scientists were defining the discourse and leading the implementation of data analytics. Many other disciplines found themselves playing catch up, unfamiliar with lingo related to algorithmic processing and underexposed to advanced methods of software programming.

Historical practices of data collection and analysis common in social sciences and the humanities, for example, were outshone by powerful new computing tools – and by the practitioners who wielded them. An "interdisciplinary" encounter about data analytics during that period might have sounded something like this:

Computer Scientist: *I've crunched the data and I've come up with a model that predicts consumer behavior.*

Social Scientist: *What do you mean by "crunched?"*

CS: *Well, I created an algorithm to process information from social media data sets about buying trends and developed a model of purchasing probability.*

SS: *And how does the algorithm work?*

CS: *Basically, it breaks the data down into computable elements and executes a finite sequence of unambiguous, digitally implementable instructions.*

SS: *But people are complex, surveying is compli-*
                cated, and sociological data is often ambiguous
                and contradictory.
CS: *The logic of the algorithm simplifies the problem*
                and removes the ambiguities.
SS: *That's what worries me.*

This is a caricature, of course, but such misalignments of vocabulary and objectives were features of the interdisciplinary landscape at that time. Computer scientists weren't giving enough consideration to the inherent complexities and limitations of certain types of data they received from non-scientific contexts such as Facebook. Social scientists, on the other hand, were uncertain about how to process such data and how to analyze the environments from which it was collected. Although sociologists were reluctant to formulate conclusions based on that data, computer scientists proceeded with computational analyses, often failing to account for the concerns of their social scientist colleagues.

Such culture clashes among disciplines certainly occurred before the era of big data, but the speed at which the field of data analytics was developing far outpaced the growth of interdisciplinary understanding and collaboration. Not surprisingly, many scholars in social-science disciplines were wary of some of the conclusions being reached by their colleagues in computer science and data analytics.

Cultural mismatches notwithstanding, the urgency of real-world challenges continued to draw many of us into interdisciplinary/multidisciplinary efforts. The more we tried to work together, the more clearly we understood that systematic analyses of data from a variety of realms would be essential to crafting equitable and sustainable solutions. We all agreed that the big problems of our age didn't belong to any single discipline, and neither did the data.

Facing Existing Disciplinary Headwinds

Despite everyone's best intentions, sustaining meaningful multidisciplinary research, teaching, and problem-solving often felt like sailing into a stiff headwind. As discussed earlier, the vast majority of incentives within academia – including jobs, space, equipment, research funding, student recruitment, publishing opportunities, and societal recognition – are organized and dispensed through established disciplines. Interesting, relevant, and urgent problems that fall within the bounds of discrete domains are numerous, if not infinite. Inevitably, departmental forces pulled people back to their home ports after temporary forays into collaborative waters.

Fortunately, for those of us whose work increasingly pointed toward multidisciplinary engagement, MIT extended an opportunity to build a new kind of transdisciplinary vehicle that could more reliably navigate the changeable winds and uncharted oceans of multidimensional, real-world problems. What emerged, after lengthy consultations across MIT's administration, its five schools, and with kindred spirits at other leading universities and scientific entities around the world, was a pioneering research and teaching ecosystem designed to tackle the unprecedented challenges posed by large-scale, heterogeneous, interconnected data and systems.

Such systems – energy, transportation, finance, healthcare, manufacturing, social networks, voting misinformation, and religious fundamentalism, to name a few – grew out of and were reshaped by late twentieth and early twenty-first advances in smart and embedded sensors, high-speed communications, social networking, and social platforms enabling real-time decision capabilities. Unfortunately, the rapid evolution of those systems in the developed world far outpaced our societies' abilities to comprehend, much less countermand, the unintended negative consequences of those advances.

We also perceived that academia, industry, and government were failing to intentionally deploy the immense power of new and rapidly evolving complex systems in ways that promoted the fulfillment of enduring universal human values. Our conviction was and still is that those failures resulted more from a lack of attention and comprehension than from malintent and market-skewing shareholder capitalism. As a result, the advisors, supporters, and founders of the new IDSS discipline coalesced around the ambition of holistically, systematically, and scientifically addressing the promises and pitfalls associated with technologically enabled complex systems.

A Better Framework for Data-to-Decision Collaborations: The IDSS Triangle

The model my IDSS colleagues and I began to formulate at MIT in 2014 grew out of the convergence of three rising pools of

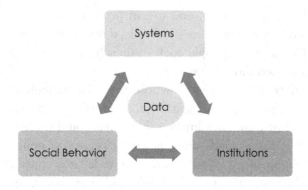

Figure 4.1 The IDSS Triangle

data – scientific, economic, and systems engineering data (common in physical systems and well documented in academia and industry); institutional data (global in scope, aggregated from the outcomes of various organizational interventions, and reliant on existing mechanisms); and data on social interactions (individual in scale but newly available via social media in mass quantities). The societal challenges that interested us in areas such as finance, energy, urbanization, social networks, and personal and public health, typically hinge on the interactions among these three nodes of the IDSS Triangle (Figure 4.1). When tackling challenges related to biases on a digital platform such as Facebook, the Triangle compels us to investigate the systemic operations of the platform, how people interact with the platform and each other, and the various policies and regulations is paramount to understand how such platforms can impact various communities. Later in this chapter, you'll find a more detailed description of how the Triangle influenced our response to the COVID-19 pandemic.

The question before us was how to establish a set of transdisciplinary principles that would enable us to tackle the complex task of deciphering interactions within our Triangle. We agreed that for almost every problem of interest to us, we must be able to collect data deliberately, make good and reliable predictions, and understand systemic fragility, bias, resilience, and security. We also need to address causality versus correlations, ensure sustainability, define the interaction architecture of people and systems associated with the problem, and propose ethical solutions that promote justice and privacy.

We recognized, as well, that we couldn't build an academic unit around the solving of societal challenges, which are infinite in number and would comprise an amorphous, ceaselessly evolving set of disciplines for each particular problem. Instead, we committed ourselves to a data-to-decisions framework that would incorporate the most effective tools, methods, and technologies from engineering/computing and the social sciences for solving real-world problems.

Our vision for better person-machine collaborations centers on conducting research and training students in human-centered and socially centered (i.e., collective human behavior) data science. Rather than designing and building machines to think for us, we want to demonstrate how AI, ML, and similar technologies can help us think deeper and more broadly about a wide range of complex, systemic problems. Human judgment must remain an essential element of every equation, but we must continually up our game with higher-quality information and a clearer understanding of what the data signify.

Data for the People

Simply stated, we founded IDSS in 2014 to leverage data about individuals and systems for the benefit of people. Or – if you are partial to a more academic characterization – we dedicated ourselves to the modeling and prediction of systemic behavior, performance, and risk; system design and architecture; and advocacy of social welfare, sustainability, and resilience. We recognized that we needed to consider equity and systemic bias by accounting for the humanity of individuals. Our hope was that our students would drive the development of new solutions while being cognizant of all those dimensions.

In our initial communication to the MIT administration regarding the establishment of IDSS, we committed to rooting our methodologies in the intersecting domains of statistics, information and decision sciences, as well as human and institutional behaviors. We also undertook to actively involve domain experts who would be essential to comprehend the multifaceted aspects of the intricate systems that gripped our attention.

Although professionals in these specific fields will grasp the implications of our transdisciplinary approach, a typical layperson may not. Earlier in the book, we discussed statistics, so here, we should elucidate the notions behind information and decision sciences. Traditionally, information and decision sciences revolve around deciphering the information inherent in data – a resource that can be extracted to serve diverse objectives such as learning, decision-making, and data compression. The field is deeply entrenched in probabilistic models, spanning both static and dynamic contexts, optimization methodologies, and the theories of decision-making and control. Some endeavors center on fundamental boundaries – that is, the constraints of what's unattainable – while others concentrate on algorithms, the pathways to what is attainable. From my perspective, statistics, information, and decision sciences synergistically facilitate the foundational principles of the data-to-decisions paradigm – the essence of AI.

Human and institutional behaviors encompass dimensions within social sciences, humanity, and economics that shed light on the interplay between data, systems, and the broader populace. Central to this understanding is the recognition of theories that underpin social reasoning, the foundational aspects of micro and macroeconomics, as well as the functioning of financial and governmental establishments. Given that our data and systems inherently originate in human actions and are harnessed to create solutions for societal needs, it's imperative to adopt a perspective that extends beyond mere utility when addressing complex challenges. Naturally, when formulating policies – an arena that serves as the testing ground for insights from social sciences and the humanities – it becomes essential to incorporate these broader viewpoints.

This mode of thinking will manifest uniquely across various domains. Crafting an algorithmic diagnostic tool for cancer, for instance, necessitates a distinct approach to aspects such as modeling, precision, and data management, which differs markedly from the considerations required for a tool catering to customer service in a digital realm. Likewise, the approach diverges significantly when tackling a reinforcement-learning solution for the challenge of nuclear fusion. The intersection of multiple specialized fields offers a significant opening to cultivate a versatile student – one who can be deeply rooted in a specific domain while embracing this innovative perspective concerning data and systems.

We expressed our ambitions with a three-pronged diagram we refer to as "The Triangle." It depicts the dynamic interactions among physical and engineered systems, individual social behavior, and social institutions. The multidirectional arrows of our diagram represent the complex, multifaceted interactions of the three nodes. Data sit at the connective tissue that bears the imprint of all three nodes.

Probabilistic thinking, statistics, and decisions under uncertainty provide a framework for the abstractions used in modeling complex phenomena. These tools employ rigorous methods to assess the quality of the data, models, and inference. The IDSS Triangle codifies elements of complexity in societal challenges within domains where heterogeneous data is collected on various components of the Triangle. Such data may be incomplete, have different time scales, and may not be time-stamped or space-stamped in a natural way.

Tailoring the approach to a particular challenge using probabilistic and statistical thinking can help us formulate the questions needed to address that challenge. This does not result in a universal solution that we can apply to every challenge. Rather, it gives us a way of thinking about each complex challenge that facilitates more productive use of heterogeneous data in modeling systems and devising solutions for that challenge.

Vignette

My overall objective in writing this book is to present the case for the emergence of this new transdiscipline – one we've termed DSS. We consider DSS to be a transdiscipline because we believe it should be embedded within all other disciplines where data and systems play a role – engineering, sciences, social sciences, and management, for example, as well as other cross-disciplinary domains within academia. The creation of a cross-university unit in the form of an Institute at MIT was essential to bringing that transdisciplinary thinking into different fields and domains. IDSS was conceived with this vision in mind.

When contemplating the emergence of the transdisciplinary field of DSS, I'm continually drawn to the analogy of the role that mathematics plays in science and engineering. While a mathematics department chiefly is concerned with forging new theories and foundations, equally integral to its mission is imparting the fundamental principles and the latest tools that are indispensable to advances in science and engineering. Interestingly, mathematics departments have willingly relinquished the sole ownership of discoveries achieved through mathematical methodologies. Mathematicians wholeheartedly appreciate the integration of their transdisciplinary contributions into the problem-solving approaches of engineers and scientists.

I'll have more to say about The Triangle and the development of IDSS as an academic unit (i.e., an institute) in later chapters. For now, I simply want to stress the importance of The Triangle in helping us to establish IDSS as a transdiscipline, rather than as a facilitator of sporadic

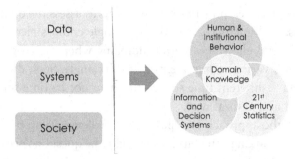

Figure 4.2 The IDSS Ecosystem

interdisciplinary/multidisciplinary collaborations. The Triangle enabled domain experts to structure their research, teaching, and policy initiatives around a shared theoretical framework and practical toolkit that could be reliably employed to understand and craft workable solutions to intractable problems such as inequality, misinformation, economic development, climate change, technology policy, and pandemic response. In that sense, I recognize a kindred spirit in philosopher and sociologist Edgar Morin, who said, "The smallest topic, however seemingly minute, can only be understood within and through its context. In fact, no problem of any significance can be perceived from within a single compartmentalized discipline – it always requires transdisciplinarity."

Our problem-solving grows out of substantive empirical and methodological breakthroughs achieved within a cohesive community of scholars and practitioners that is distinct in the history of computing. The structure of an institute enables us to bring together various domains as co-owners of this new emerging transdiscipline and naturally embeds it within their own disciplines. Hence our assertion that IDSS cannot be structured as a standalone entity. We've expressed that distinct set of interdependencies as a Ven diagram we refer to as the IDSS Ecosystem (Figure 4.2).

Responding to a Pandemic in Real-Time: Case in Point

The onset of the COVID-19 global pandemic in 2020 threw scientific, political, and economic institutions into turmoil. As reported cases increased exponentially and unpredictable human health effects proliferated, policymakers were confronted with a very difficult task – make decisions about how best to save and preserve lives in a highly uncertain environment. With only limited and noisy data, the scientific community went to work in order to extract as much information as possible about the virus and its contagion. Anti-science communities (a nontrivial subset of societies worldwide) went into denial. They blamed the scientific community for issuing mixed messages – including the variable guidance about wearing masks.

Faced with dearth of data about this metastasizing threat, countries implemented various levels of lockdowns. Simultaneously, data scientists and epidemiologists raced to improve their models of the contagion in order to answer crucial questions such as: Do lockdowns deliver a causal effect on the decline of infections? Can we predict the apex of the infection curve as a function of lockdowns? To reach useful conclusions about these and other questions, many scientists relied on hospitalization data. Although the data were limited and noisy, experts produced significant insights about the mechanisms of the contagion.

A media and public policy battle soon arose, however, among healthcare specialists on one side and business, economic, and social specialists on the other. The economic consequences of lockdowns were severe, and the debates were heated. Is it better to save as many lives as possible and resurrect the economy in the aftermath, or do you minimize lockdowns to protect the livelihoods on which society depends and accept a certain level of mortality up front? We must remember that – even in the throes of a global pandemic –scientific discovery remains a process. Given a particular quantity of data sets, we may resort initially to a severe lockdown and then slowly evolve that decision as we learn more. Anti-scientists use the evolution of decisions as an indicator of failure of science when, to the contrary, that is the very nature –and greatest strength – of science.

The challenges posed by COVID-19 serve as excellent examples of the Triangle. The biological aspect of the virus, including its size and ability to attach, forms part of the system's data set. The interaction between people is a consequence of social data, and government policies and interventions constitute institutional data. To address any of these challenges, it is essential to consider the interactions between all these components.

A Testing and Vaccination Moonshot

Given past experiences with viral epidemics, experts generally agreed on one point – vaccination was the most urgent and effective intervention. Some even compared it with the twentieth-century program to land a human on the moon. The global scientific community went into high gear and produced vaccines within the span of a year. An impressive feat in its own right, this accomplishment also resulted in the acceleration of new technologies (mRNA, for instance) that will likely help solve future medical and public health challenges.

Even before the vaccines were ready, the scientific community also produced effective rapid tests that helped mitigate the spread of the virus. Tests, which were created and deployed at unprecedented speed and scale, gave us a reliable tool for temporarily removing infected individuals from the network of contagion via quarantine. This was essential because many infected individuals were younger, largely asymptomatic, and unlikely to self-quarantine. One key to using tests effectively was to determine the optimal testing rate – a classic exercise in control and decision theory. Control theory experts at IDSS and around the world helped craft approaches for testing protocols that guided the work of public health officials.

Leveraging Data about the Contagion Network

The methodology related to testing protocols is instructive – and an excellent example of the IDSS Triangle in action. Contagion occurs in a network in which people physically interact, and lockdowns reduce those network interactions. Because the speed at which the virus spreads can be measured scientifically (biologically, it depends on the size of the virus plus its ability to attach to molecules in the body), we can estimate the virus's reproductive factor (Ro) by monitoring data on the number of infections in a given environment.

Ro enables us to calculate the average number of people a single infected person can infect during the time they are contagious. The number depends upon the setting. In a dorm in which many students interact, Ro can be as high as 10. By contrast, Ro can be less than 1 in casual outdoor interactions. The implications of this spread are significant. If Ro = 2, for example, the first infected person can infect an average of two other people, who intern infect four others, and so on. By estimating the resulting exponential growth, you can quantify the effective rate for testing within a community. The goal is to test and quarantine infected individuals faster than the rate at which they are infecting others, which will reduce Ro to less than 1.

When MIT successfully implemented a testing/quarantining strategy in 2020 based on this methodology, many other higher education institutions did the same. The implementation unfolded across multiple levels: in the Fall of 2020, over half of the students returned to campus. They were organized into Pods of 8–10 individuals with restricted external interactions, limited in-person group meetings, and a heightened emphasis on utilizing outdoor spaces. Students underwent testing three times a week, a frequency determined by calculations considering the spread of COVID and student interactions. In contrast, faculty and staff were tested once a week. Those testing positive among students were quarantined in a separate dormitory, while infected faculty and staff were required to wait for a negative test result or more than 10 days after symptoms before returning. Despite the apparent challenges, this strategy proved remarkably effective, fostering continued interaction among students, faculty, and staff.

We realized the full impact of the strategy when the IDSS faculty collaborated with NIH/CIMIT to create the "whentotest.org" app. My colleague Professor Peko Hosoi recognized the importance of simplifying our theory to have a meaningful influence. While the app represented a technical achievement, its straightforwardness demonstrated a keen understanding of people's needs during the pandemic. Details of the technology and its implications are covered in 2024 *Accelerating Diagnostics in a Time of Crisis*: The Response to COVID-19 and a Roadmap for Future Pandemics by editors Steven C. Schachter and Wade E. Bolton.

Public Policies and the IDSS Triangle

In the 2023 article "Implicit feedback policies for COVID-19: why 'zero-COVID' policies remain elusive," my colleagues Ali Jadbabaie and Devavrat Shah, in collaboration with their IDSS student Arnab Sarkar, found that publishing data about the total number of current infections in a given region produced a healthy feedback effect. Essentially, people who consumed public reporting about a high number of infections in their locale were more careful about their activities within that contagion network. They exercised greater self-restraint in their interactions with other people in their daily lives.

The implications of this finding highlight a fundamental characteristic of the IDSS Triangle – the intertwined nature of DSS. As the study by Jadbabaie, Shah, and Sarkar illustrates, the effectiveness of a policy intervention arises from the interaction among the science of the contagion, social and economic structures and behaviors, and the trade-offs embedded in the policy of testing and quarantining. We must consider all these components when seeking to assess and design the most effective policy responses.

The Triangle also helps us to assess the ongoing effects of a policy intervention and adjust as needed. In the example above, the compromise between human versus economic health turned out to have a major, likely unintended, bias against historically under-resourced communities. People suffered greater harm from these policies in homes where average incomes were lower, where employment was manual, where healthcare was less accessible, and where the number of individuals per household was higher than average. At IDSS, we believe The Triangle is essential to addressing issues of fairness, which I'll be talking about more in the coming chapters.

5 COMPLEXITY VERSUS RELEVANCE
The Power of Abstractions

In the first episode of the Netflix television series *Abstract: The Art of Design*, illustrator Christoph Niemann talks about how he achieves the right level of abstraction in his graphic design work. "Each idea," he says, "requires a very specific amount of information. Sometimes it's a lot – a lot of details, a lot of realism – and sometimes it's really like just this one line, the one pixel. But each idea has one moment on that scale."

To illustrate his point, Niemann cites the example of a heart as an abstraction or symbol for the idea of love. If you depict it with the ultimate simplification of a red square, he says, "nobody knows what you're talking about, so it totally falls flat." If, on the other hand, you use super-realism and draw a lifelike human heart, the last thing anybody would ever think about is love. But somewhere in between those two points on what he calls his "Abstract-O-Meter" is the two-dimensional, graphic Valentine's Day shape we recognize as "just right to transport this idea of the symbol for love." The result is an infinitely varied and complex phenomenon – love – distilled to a communicative essence.

In physics, simple models are abstractions of reality. Newton's gravitation law is an extremely pared-down representation of motion that does not account for the dependence of space and time. While this model has limitations at high speed, it is one of the most intuitive and powerful tools of physics. The bottom line is that abstractions help us build better and more intuitive understandings of real-world systems and enable us to make very good decisions in a timely fashion.

Abstractions are common in our everyday lives because they are instinctive, and neuroscience confirms that such thinking is crucial to human cognition. But when it comes to modeling, analyzing – and hopefully improving – the complex systems that determine the physical, social, and economic health of human societies, achieving the right level of abstraction requires quite a bit more intention and expertise. I contend that there is no systematic approach to deriving an abstraction; instead, in my view, it is a manifestation of the creativity of our minds.

Information Theory and the Power of Abstraction

The creation of information theory as a discipline is a good example of how abstractions help us solve difficult problems in complex systems. One of the core challenges tackled by the mathematician, electrical engineer, and cryptographer Claude Shannon in the 1930s and 1940s was to model the problem of separating, or "smoothing," core signals from extraneous noise (e.g., in a fire-control communications network). Another problem was to extract the correct meaning of a transmission from an encrypted set of signals designed to confound everyone except the person or persons with the key for decoding the message. Shannon used fundamental ideas from probability theory to define the limits of uncertainty in those digital transmissions. Shannon's primary goal was to formulate a theory for transmitting digital data through channels affected by noise in order to send a digital message through a noisy channel and reliably recover it at the receiving end, either exactly or with a high probability of accuracy.

Consider the following scenario in which we aim to transmit a randomly generated sequence of binary signals with values 0, 1. Let's assume that the channel flips each binary signal 25% of the time. The objective is to ensure nearly precise retrieval of any sequence at the receiving end. Naturally, a straightforward solution exists – transmit each binary signal multiple times. The receiver can employ a majority rule to correctly identify the transmitted binary signal that, with high probability, yields the correct answer. But there's a trade-off. This approach results in a low transmission rate. In situations where high transmission rates are crucial, such as real-time video streaming, the approach introduces significant latency.

Shannon abstracted this challenging problem by defining a distinct notion of information.

Information, as modeled in Shannon's 1948 article "A Mathematical Theory of Communication," is not a function of what you *do* say but rather what you *could* say. As such, it reflects the amount of freedom a person has in choosing any particular communication reduced by any limiting rules of the written language being represented.

Shannon used this approach to create a mathematical formalism that quantified the amount of information contained in a given source of messages. He hypothesized a random alphabet with a known distribution as a source of messages from which a particular letter is picked with some probability. In a similar vein, we can think of a collection of English words, each picked with some frequency, as a message source. In Shannon's hypothesis, the entropy of the source was shown to play a very important role in characterizing the shortest codes representing messages in the sources, a problem Shannon referred to as "source coding." The concept of entropy is important in the hypothesis because it measures the degree of randomness in a given alphabet. In a binary alphabet with only two letters (say 0, 1), for example, the entropy is small if one of these letters occurs with high probability. The maximum randomness is when they both have equal probabilities.

When Shannon applied his methodology to the English language, he showed how it could reduce by nearly five times the amount of digital signaling necessary for a reliable transmission. (Note that the concept of a source, as depicted by Shannon, is in itself an abstraction of real messages in communication systems.) Once messages were coded, they were transmitted through a noisy channel. In that scenario, the redundancy approach I mentioned earlier would not be efficient.

Shannon's work on channel coding described the optimal approach to creating just enough redundancy in a signal to completely recover it at the other end of transmission, giving mathematicians and engineers one of their most powerful examples of abstraction. Although coding methods in digital communication must account for many additional factors such as transmission delays, it was Shannon's abstraction that enabled the digital communications revolution. It paved the way for such disciplines and technologies as computer networks, adaptive and anticipatory systems, informatics, cybernetics, AI, and ML, among many others. Shannon's theory of information also exemplified a methodology that enables us to effectively tackle problems in complex, dynamic systems when faced with noisy, imperfect, incomplete, or overwhelming amounts of data. Today, it is quite common to conceive of levels of abstraction when designing the architecture of complex systems, from the physical layer all the way to the application layer.

Systems, Interconnections, and Equilibria: More Abstraction

Scientists and engineers have made tremendous progress in discovery and design by breaking systems down into smaller components, such as the individual organs of the body or the engines and wings of a plane. A challenge arises, however, when trying to understand the complex behaviors that emerge from reassembling those smaller components. Although studying the liver in isolation provides valuable insights, a person's overall well-being is determined by the integration of multiple organs. Similarly, individual banks may have distinct strategies, but systemic failures result from the interactions among multiple financial institutions. Even executing excellent designs for individual components of a plane is not enough to ensure that it flies well. The performance of a fully assembled aircraft depends on the interconnected functionality of all the parts. Social behaviors and viral pandemics also exemplify the influence of interconnections in the overall outcomes of complex systems.

An essential aspect of interconnections is the presence of feedback systems. In an airplane, a feedback system could measure the position of the airplane and then, through some control design, adjust the power of the thrusters in order to keep the plane in a steady position. In our bodies, we have numerous feedback systems that adjust our sugar level or keep our internal temperature constant.

Feedback systems, whether natural or designed, help maintain equilibrium within a given context. Equilibrium represents a state where a system behaves in a highly predictable manner. An airplane's control system, for example, is designed to keep the plane stable (i.e., in equilibrium) at a specific pitch angle. In infectious diseases, natural stabilizing feedback mechanisms might emerge when more people get sick, causing them to stay home and reduce infection rates. In domains such as economics, demand and supply are stabilized through pricing mechanisms. When demand increases, prices rise. Price hikes, in turn, reduce demand and generate a more stable state in the market.

The general concept of equilibrium provides a simplified way to think about interconnections and complexity in systems such as aircraft, markets, and food demand. We often consider factors that can push systems away from equilibrium and intervene to mitigate these deviations. In the specific case of COVID-19, natural feedback loops were eliminated by the fact that we had so many asymptomatic carriers, which in turn created the necessity for additional interventions above and beyond self-isolation. Through intervention and feedback, we can minimize the uncertainty caused by these deviations and work with approximations and simplified models to better address complexity.

Within the domain of robust control and decision theory, researchers address uncertainty within abstracted models using feedback mechanisms that incorporate actual observed outcomes from past decisions. Strategies can thus be crafted to optimize robustness when real-world behaviors deviate from modeled expectations. In the context of an airplane navigating severe turbulence, for example, the aerodynamics may exhibit greater unpredictability than a model predicts. By skillfully designing a feedback control system, a researcher or engineer can effectively manage and mitigate the impact of uncertain effects. Such advanced methods in robust control theory offer valuable insights that extend to broader societal decision-making challenges.

Vignette

Computation Meets Statistics: One rewarding aspect of the IDSS community is the extent to which practical and theoretical research – and researchers from different domains – thrive in proximity to one another. This is evident in the work of statistician Philippe Rigollet and information theorist Guy Bresler, both IDSS faculty members. For a considerable period in the recent past, these two domains were mostly disconnected and lacked a clear bridge between them. This mattered because certain statistical challenges pose greater difficulties than others. While information theory offers a framework for characterizing the information embedded in a noisy data set, and thus provides a basis for evaluating what is learnable, it is often the case that computational complexity imposes an additional constraint on learning.

In the cases of both Rigollet and Bresler, their work spans that gap by using insights from both domains to address the complexity that arises from the presence of two fundamental factors: the volume of data required for model learning (sample complexity) and the computational resources needed for the learning process (computational complexity). Historically, statisticians have focused primarily on questions related to sample complexity (addressed in statistical learning theory literature), while computer scientists have concentrated on assessing the computational complexity of problems and their categorization. What was lacking was a unifying mathematical concept that could harmonize these two aspects, enabling the derivation of valuable insights into various statistical learning questions. This abstract mathematical concept was subsequently identified as the pursuit of discovering a hidden clique within a graph.

If you are given a randomly generated graph of nodes and links and you are told that there is a clique (a fully connected subgraph) embedded in the graph, how would you find it? More important, if you are not a theoretical mathematician, why should you care? It turns out that if you are interested in using large data sets to predict the probable behavior of large and complex real-life systems (e.g., the community spread of an airborne virus), successfully identifying a planted clique has immense potential value.

The utilization of the planted clique as a tool for understanding the relationship between statistical challenge and computational difficulty is a unique and powerful abstraction. One can appreciate this by thinking of the planted clique of a given size as a signal and the random graph as noise. Separating this signal from the noise without additional information will require an exhaustive search for all cliques, which would be prohibitively time-consuming. But can some statistical information reduce this search? Intuitively, if the clique is of a large size (e.g., larger than natural cliques in the random graph), then it is likely that you can find it quickly just by starting with nodes of large degrees. That intuition turns out to be correct, and we think of this condition as a large signal-to-noise ratio. Of course, one has to quantify exactly what a large clique really means.

Alternatively, if the size of the clique is too small (e.g., smaller than natural cliques in the random graph), then it appears to be impossible to separate the signal from the noise, regardless of what algorithm you use. This is the result of confusion between the embedded clique and the natural ones, and it corresponds to the limit of what is learnable from data. Again, one has to quantify what is meant by a small clique. My colleagues Rigollet and Bressler addressed exactly this issue and were able to provide the regime (in terms of the size of the clique as a function of the size of the random graph) where one end represented the statistical limit of learning, and the other end represented what is easily learnable. The regime in between represented problems that are learnable but do not have a known simple algorithm for finding the clique. This approach provided a complete characterization of these complexity tradeoffs.

> *Bresler examined this problem further and was intrigued – how far could he stretch such an analysis to address common problems in high dimensional statistics such as the celebrated principal component analysis (PCA)? His transformative work at the intersection of three fields – statistics, theory of computing, and information theory – is exactly what we envisioned our young faculty would be doing to support the new statistics emerging in the twenty-first century. It's beyond the scope of this book to describe fully how Bresler did this. If you are interested in a deeper dive, I highly recommend the in-depth 2018 paper "Reducibility and Computational Lower Bounds for Problems with Planted Sparse Structure," which describes how Bresler and his collaborators solved this problem.*

The Wider Landscape of Uncertainty and Imperfection

Although information theory has had a broad and enduring impact on the digitization of society, its original application was focused on a purely engineering problem. Today, our imperative is to intertwine significant engineering challenges with social science phenomena and public and technology policy initiatives.

It is nearly impossible to solve a complex societal problem without zeroing in on the most consequential subset of elements within a given system. This simplification process applies as much to devising and adjusting effective public health policy in the midst of a global pandemic as it does to the engineering and siting of a nuclear power plant. Both problems comprise countless details – and you could devote countless hours accounting for every element in those systems without ever arriving at an actionable solution.

The pursuit of a workable abstraction – that is, the simplest model that explains the behavior of a system in a particular context – is a fundamental principle of mathematical system theory and statistics, but it is historically less a feature of domains concerned with human and institutional behaviors, with the exception of certain aspects of theoretical economics. That's why domain experts from the humanities and social sciences are essential to data-driven team efforts to solve our most daunting challenges. In forging those collaborations, however, we on the data science side must resist the temptation to force our nonengineering colleagues to think like engineers. We must, if you will, transition from a form of totalitarian (and utilitarian) thinking to incorporate more humanistic, artistic, and ethical considerations.

The Role of Abstraction in Policymaking

Consider, for example, the subprime mortgage crisis and the Great Recession of 2008. It was not possible to understand, predict, or mitigate the systemic risk or cascaded failures of that global financial-system crisis solely from observations of past data. This rare event was heavily influenced by the financial protocols, underlying government policies, and numerous incentives that had been created to influence people's behaviors.

Data were available for some parts of this complex system – and different data were available to different decision-makers in the system – but few, if any, key actors had all the data needed to address the crisis coherently before, during, and immediately after the crash. It is impossible to gauge the extent to which an abstraction of the global financial system could have limited, or even prevented, some of the damage. I suggest, however, that a more useful predictor of potential problems may emerge from collaborative modeling.

Although most corporate leaders failed to anticipate the crisis, many were cognizant of the potential for cascading failure within their industries. When the CEO of Ford Motor Company requested emergency government action to prevent General Motors from failing, the motive was not a desire to preserve one of its fiercest rivals for the sake of competition. Rather, Ford's leaders understood that if GM failed, so would many of the intermediate suppliers on which Ford also depended. GM's collapse could very well have put Ford at grave risk of failure, as well. Such interdependencies within complex global systems underscore the need for a more rigorous understanding of systemic issues (i.e., issues emerging from interconnections) in general. The fact that the 2020 global pandemic triggered massive supply chain and travel breakdowns reinforces the urgency of developing new tools for analyzing and predicting large-scale systemic failures.

Wrapping Our Heads around Congestion

At the beginning of this book, I touched on traffic delays as a negative consequence of a complex system that has huge implications for our physical, mental, and economic wellbeing – individually and collectively. Our day-to-day experiences of ever-worsening congestion suggest that we have largely failed on a societal level to solve or even lessen this problem. Might abstraction help us manage those systems more effectively? A look at four key components of the overall challenge – individuals' behaviors, economic costs, control levers, and decision-makers – may shed some light on the possibilities.

Within a network of connected roads, congestion can be fairly well modeled mathematically using partial differential equations that describe how traffic densities change over time as a function of traffic input. We affect such networks when we drive to our jobs as well as the various amenities available in our towns, cities, and regions. Some of our travel is dictated by the clock (e.g., to and from work), while other travel occurs on more flexible schedules (e.g., recreational activities). We may choose to travel by personal vehicle, ride-sharing, or various modes of public transportation. Needs, incentives, feedback from real-time congestion, and herding behaviors also influence our decisions. Models of our collective impact on a transit system must account for all these factors, and such models are very complicated and not collectively agreed upon.

From a cost perspective, municipalities, and states strive to minimize the short- and long-term economic impacts of congestion – lost job productivity, diminished property values, displacement of available housing, business relocations, and environmental degradation, to name a few. These harms occur on multiple time scales and with varying degrees of interdependence. The potential control levers available to authorities at local levels include real-time traffic signals, speed limits, toll incentives and penalties, and one- and two-way travel directives. These levers operate at local levels. On a regional scale, authorities may construct more alternative routes, deny access to certain types of vehicles at certain times of day, or impose penalties for excess CO_2 emissions.

Complicating these factors is the wide spectrum of decision-makers within the system. Engineers make infrastructure design decisions to control flow and maximize throughput. Individual travelers make strategic personal decisions to satisfy their primary objectives (e.g., travel from point A to point B in the shortest amount of time). Any person's assessment of which actions will best serve that objective, however, may vary from day to day and often may be counterproductive. Local and regional authorities, for their part, seek to establish policies and incentives they hope will promote equitable access to healthy, productive, and rewarding living conditions.

When Individual Knowledge Becomes a Systemic Problem

Embedded GPS systems in passenger vehicles represent a potentially confounding factor in traffic congestion. While those systems provide valuable traffic information to individual drivers, they can have a negative impact by routing a critical mass of drivers toward the same alternative route, resulting in new congestion points. Newer generations of GPS systems aim to overcome this limitation by incorporating individual driver preferences and providing personalized recommendations for alternative routes. That technological advance opens up opportunities for municipalities to utilize information design as a tool for battling congestion in their regions. Information design, in that context, refers to deliberately using the design and presentation of private information to influence the decisions and behavior of multiple individuals. By leveraging that approach, municipalities and states can enhance their control over traffic congestion at the individual level.

The control and transportation communities named this research area cyber-physical systems. The cyber component is created from the GPS digital platform as well as sophisticated, real-time dynamic controls for toll, traffic light, and speed regulation. Those components typically are concerned with the physical transportation system but do not attempt to incentivize individual behavior. Information design, by contrast, focuses on providing information that will nudge people to behave in a way that is good for the overall system while not compromising their individual objectives. This emerging and dynamic area of research presents many challenges, however. Modeling each of these complicated subsystems is extremely difficult and merging all the components into one overarching representation is nearly impossible. Even if such a model could be created, the result would be so unwieldy that it would have little utility for policymakers seeking to design equitable systems that incentivize societally beneficial behaviors.

No One-Abstraction-Fits-All Solution

Unfortunately, we lack a foolproof formula for creating comprehensive abstractions. On the problem of congestion, every discipline is likely to view the system through a distinct lens. A computer scientist or control theorist might create a multilayered model that separates the detailed operations of the transportation system from the higher-level decisions discussed above. By combining the layers, the model could theoretically describe the effects of people's interactions with the operations of the system. Across a short timescale, abstracted models of the impact of tolls on driving behaviors have proven to be very effective in managing congestion.

Looking at the same system, environmental scientists may arrive at a different abstraction. They may examine the long-term effect of a particular policy (e.g., aggregating models of traffic and pollution over decades) to assess the impact of a given policy on the environment. Urban planners might use similar aggregate models to study the impact on city expansion or migration. And economists may evaluate the effects of adding a carbon tax on system users. Their primary objective would likely be to understand how policies affect the equilibrium of the macroeconomy such as highlighting how the carbon tax could alter other related operations that may ultimately result in a loss of efficiency or some other metric.

Each approach outlined above could provide insight into key aspects of this complex system. At the same time, each discipline would run the risk of ignoring some essential component that is key to improving the overall system. Inventing ways of combining all relevant analyses is the crux of successfully analyzing complex systems and making effective policies. This is what we are attempting to model with the IDSS Triangle and to implement in our ongoing research, including our doctoral program in Social and Engineering Systems (SES). I'll talk more about that and other IDSS programs in Chapter 7.

How Abstraction Shaped IDSS

For systems and society, one important implication of abstraction in all its forms is causality. A proposed policy or intervention must have a causal effect on the desired outcome. In the context of pharmaceutical development, for example, you would be inefficient at best, and dangerously erroneous at worst, to develop a vaccine for hepatitis C solely based on experimentation and clinical trials while foregoing a deeper dive into functions and mechanisms inside the human liver.

As noted in Chapter 4, the model that guides IDSS grew out of the convergence of data from scientific, economic, and engineering processes; data from institutional sources; and data from social interactions. The societal challenges that continue to interest us – in domains such as finance, energy, urbanization, social networks, and personal and public health – typically hinge on the interactions among those three heterogeneous data pools, and we seek to give appropriate weight to all three. Without an explicit understanding of the interactions between those components, data alone may result in vastly erroneous conclusions. Causality is certainly one dimension that can suffer greatly in the absence of such systemic dependencies. Our previous discussion in Chapter 4 on COVID-19 is a primary example of this interaction and the role of causality in assessing the impacts of interventions.

Thinking about causality played a role in leading us to structure our academic program around the Triangle. In the context of a particular domain, we observe aspects of the three elements – systems, human and social interactions, and institutional interactions – through heterogeneous data sets. Such data sets can be noisy – different resolution levels, different time scales, sparse, high dimensional, or aggregate. We need new statistical theories with which to assess causality, prediction, or systemic effects. A certain level of abstraction is necessary to get any quantifiable or testable outcomes. Such an abstraction takes us back to modeling, which requires domain experts at the heart of the analysis. It also carries with it a responsibility to stay engaged with each problem we tackle so that we can adjust any components of our abstraction that result in erroneous or counterproductive conclusions.

Our discussion earlier in this book about the abstraction of transportation systems illustrates the challenge of staying engaged and making adjustments to simplified models. To grasp the resilience of a traffic network –that is, understanding the minimum disruption capable of triggering widespread traffic cascades – engineers or researchers can create simplified mathematical models of traffic flow based on models of drivers' behaviors. They can use those models to analyze how the equilibrium shifts when there is a loss of capacity on certain roads (e.g., in the event of an accident). Their analyses may suggest real-time interventions to avert equilibria with high congestion. In tandem with any intervention, however, practitioners must evaluate the robustness of their initial solution when drivers react to the intervention with strategic behaviors that may counteract the effectiveness of the first solution.

Modeling the Wisdom of Crowds: Case in Point

In today's digitally interconnected sociocultural communities, most of our individual decisions are influenced – and sometimes determined – by the advice and actions of others. Consumer purchases, dining experiences, travel excursions, investments, and voting are among numerous choices routinely affected by the opinions and experiences of other individuals and groups. This phenomenon, first characterized as "the wisdom of crowds" by *The New Yorker* financial writer James Surowiecki in 2005, was embraced by many as one of the great promises of the internet age.

The fundamental premise of the wisdom of crowds (sometimes referred to as collective intelligence) is that large groups of people communicating with one another are smarter than an elite subset of presumed subject experts. Surowiecki attributed this capability to activities such as problem-solving, invention, decision-making, and prediction of future trends or outcomes. Although the general premise is seductive, many commentators – as well as Surowiecki himself – have identified numerous phenomena that can distort or confound the wisdom of crowds.

One confounding phenomenon of particular interest in relation to data science is herding. In daily life, herding behaviors are ubiquitous, notoriously difficult to model, and sometimes catastrophic. A crowded restaurant, for example, can draw in passersby on the assumption that the food must be good. An in-demand product can attract additional buyers based solely on its popularity. On the more disastrous end of the spectrum, a bank run can cascade into the collapse of a financial system. In each case, the momentum of herding behaviors may quickly outpace or run contrary to underlying facts that should inform the crowd's actions.

Herd Decisions Are Not Wholly Rational

When a typical consumer decides what laptop to buy, they compare the features of various options, digest marketing material, sample expert reviews, and perhaps most important, consider what others in their social and professional networks buy. Their decision, in turn, affects what the next person in their network decides to buy. In this way, the decision-making process becomes a fluid mix of rational thinking and psychological and emotional bias that can be difficult to quantify.

The mix of rational and emotional decision-making becomes even murkier when people decide how to cast their ballots for president. On the rational side of the equation, voters consider competing candidates' policy positions, past records, and analyses from pundits on a variety of issues. On the psychological/emotional side, the opinions of voters' contacts in social and professional networks hold sway along with emotion-based appeals from campaigns and media influencers. When a vote is finally cast, the typical voter is likely incapable of accurately identifying to what extent each of those many factors influenced their final decision. How much more complex, then, for a researcher to predict or model the effect of herding across the entire electorate.

Another important factor to consider when analyzing herding scenarios is whether the actions of individuals within the herd influence the underlying properties of the object or entity being acted upon. Our instincts and experience help us understand this phenomenon in relation to restaurants and bank runs. As a restaurant, for example, gains popularity and grows more crowded, the cuisine may or may not improve as a result. The herd cannot be directly credited with changing the object (cuisine). In the case of a bank run, however, cascading withdrawals by the herd can degrade the health of a bank until it fails.

Although both of these examples seem relatively straightforward, neither is simple to model for the purposes of analyzing or predicting. The data any one individual collects about a product or an institution is quite heterogeneous, possibly correlated, and potentially erroneous. Alongside that, the influence of a person's network on their final decision will vary depending on the strength of the connections across the network. Add to that the simultaneous and mostly unknowable activity across the networks of all the people in the first person's network, and you have a lot of factors you can't easily quantify. Finally, the process of aggregating these various types of information may not be rational, and each person's assessment of the riskiness of an action will factor into the final decision.

Extracting Wisdom from a Herd

Despite the complications described above, researchers continue to search for the wisdom of crowds in the midst of herding phenomena. Engineering intuition suggests that we should abstract out as many lesser effects as possible and focus on one or two components of the problem. One approach to simplifying relies on three assumptions. First, assume that the decision at hand is binary and that there is a ground truth (e.g., one restaurant can be judged objectively as the best, all others less than the best). Second, assume that the data each person collects (known as the private signal) has a greater than 50% probability of being correct (i.e., the aggregate information on local restaurants favors the best restaurant for a majority of people, but not necessarily all). Third, assume that each individual's network is fixed and that any member of the network can observe all the decisions already made by network members to whom they are connected.

That third assumption incorporates an understanding that each individual observes the decisions of others in their network rather than the private signals they receive (e.g., a person observes the decisions made by their neighbors but not the information they used to make that decision). The law of large numbers guarantees that observing the independent private signals about the correct decision is sufficient for the correct aggregation to the right answer. That assertion – known as the Condorcet's Jury Theorem – was set out by David Austen-Smith and Jeffrey S. Banks in their 1996 paper "Information Aggregation, Rationality, and the Condorcet Jury Theorem" to provide a benchmark for the aggregation of information. But what about observing just the decisions?

Although this is a relatively simplified view of real-world herding behaviors, the approach yields some interesting insights. A network with good characteristics should avoid a key weakness of the so-called "star network" in which everyone is connected to a single expert whose opinion is valued by everyone in the network. If the star makes the wrong decision, herding will trend toward the wrong decision. Similarly, just observing the decisions that came before yours, you still could fall victim to a cascading series of incorrect choices and reinforce erroneous herding. A surprising aspect of this latter outcome is that it can occur even if you are able to observe the decisions that everyone made before you in the network. In other words, observing the decisions of agents on the network obscures the underlying information available in the aggregate private signals each agent receives.

It is possible, however, that if agents are able to observe all the decisions others in the network made before making their decisions, then the herd can trend toward the right decision. All it takes is a certain non-trivial number of agents to have private signals with increasing accuracy for productive learning to occur over time – a phenomenon known as unbounded rationality. The topic is thoroughly discussed by Daron Acemoglu and coauthors in the 2011 article "Bayesian Learning in Social Networks" as well as in Matthew O. Jackson's book "Social and Economic Networks." This approach to abstraction has applications in studies of systemic risk – in transportation networks, power grids, and financial systems – as well as research into cultural forces such as opinion dynamics, the evolution of social norms, and the development of consensus in social networks.

6 THE CARE AND FEEDING OF A NEW DISCIPLINE AT MIT

The fact that many critical real-world problems don't fit neatly into any one academic discipline is not a new insight. Nor are efforts to bring multiple disciplines together in ad hoc groupings to pursue effective solutions to such challenges. Within academia, however, many of those initiatives and outcomes have proved transitory, if not ephemeral, in terms of having a sustained impact on society at large. Notable exceptions to this general phenomenon in the modern era are the disciplines of molecular biology and computational genetics – both of which grew out of interdisciplinary initiatives.

Among the hurdles to sustaining multidisciplinary and interdisciplinary work are the absence of a sense of community and a coherent culture among the diverse participants in such ventures. Those factors result in, and are exacerbated by, a lack of shared journals, conferences, core topics, common knowledge, and administrative clarity typical of a robust and productive disciplinary community.

Missing, too, are the broadly shared multidisciplinary challenges and open problems that sustain research endeavors and create breakthroughs over time – despite the fact that shared problems requiring extensive data-science expertise are on the rise. This factor, however, is rapidly changing as data becomes more accessible and software is commodified. All these deficits complicate evaluation for hiring, promotion, and tenure and hamper efforts to attract such essential resources as internal and external funding, space, infrastructure, and institutional backing. Entities in industry and government often engage in interdisciplinary research, but those activities are not sufficient to create a disciplinary culture. A brief historical overview sheds light on how the MIT initiative around IDSS developed.

A Snippet of IDSS History

In December 2013, then Dean of Engineering Ian Waitz asked me to lead an initiative to conceive an academic unit rooted in systems and data science. His request didn't come out of thin air. A few years earlier, Ian invited me to join a committee (chaired by my colleague Ron Rivest) that was assessing whether the Engineering Systems Division, then approximately 15 years old, was progressing in a way that aligned with the rest of MIT. In the midst of that work, the committee shifted its focus to examine what type of entity would best serve the Institute, given the growing roles of data and systems across all domains. Our committee ultimately recommended the creation of a new entity to facilitate this transformative phenomenon. Concurrent with those efforts, Ian formed another committee to address how MIT could officially incorporate statistics into its offerings. This second endeavor was particularly urgent because MIT had been seeking a solution to that challenge for four decades.

Ian and I, in close consultation with then Associate Dean of Engineering Cindy Barnhart and in coordination with then Provost Chris Kaizer, assembled a committee of 40 faculty and staff to help delineate the blueprints for this novel entity. I recall Cindy joking at the time, "Munther is trying to kill this project by having 40 faculty members on a committee" – a quip that belied the significant challenge of reaching consensus among such a large group. We ultimately secured the endorsement of 38 committee members with two dissenters. I dedicated substantial time to comprehending the thinking of the dissenters, and for the most part, their perspectives proved to be well-founded, constructive, and efficacious to the formation of the entity.

We established four subcommittees, each with a specific focus – vision, structure, education, and statistics. These sub-committees engaged in extensive cross-discussions, tirelessly working toward a consensus on the mission and vision of the new entity. Their findings ultimately led to the emergence of the triangle concept I've discussed at some length in this book. With the vision established, the outcomes of the structure, education, and statistics sub-committees seemed to naturally align and fall into place. We reached consensus about statistics and data science being at the core of the new entity while also promoting a strong connection to the systems that generate such data. We had dissent, however, on the structure of faculty hiring (another topic I cover extensively in this book). Our 40-member committee produced a blueprint and submitted our report ("Report on the Formation of a New Entity in the Areas of Complex and Socio-technical Systems, Information and Decision Systems, and Statistics") to the provost for evaluation.

Marty Schmidt, the newly appointed provost at that time, released the report to the MIT community to gather feedback, and we received plenty. I responded to as many comments as possible and adjusted the structure of the entity as appropriate. In the fall of 2014, we soft-launched the New Entity using that name as a temporary title. I devoted the next 12 months to assembling a leadership team and, along with those colleagues, translating our visionary concept into practical reality.

Choosing an appropriate permanent name proved to be a challenge. Initially, we considered (and soon abandoned) the Institute for Statistics and Information Sciences (ISIS) – for obvious reasons. I suggested the Institute for Data and Systems, with the possible addition of "for the benefit of society," because I wanted to convey our strong societal focus. When I consulted Martha Eddison Sieniewicz, a communications consultant to then MIT President Rafael Reif, she suggested IDSS. Nearly everyone involved in the naming process found Martha's variation appealing – and we had our name!

DSS as a transdiscipline is anchored in statistical thinking, information and decision systems, abstractions, and ethical concerns. To grow this new transdisciplinary activity into a thriving academic discipline, the culture must promote deep engagements with domain experts. This sense of this culture was not fully formed at the creation of IDSS. Rather, it emerged through the process of thinking about the foundations of what we were building and the structure and programs that would promote collaborations.

IDSS Antecedents and Foundations

To place the launch of IDSS in the proper context, it's important to briefly describe the MIT antecedents that shaped the foundation for IDSS programs and activities. The DSS transdiscipline emerged not as a break with the past but as the latest fruition of many intersecting historical and present-day academic initiatives at MIT. That context is key to understanding how we choose to proceed.

Chapter 2 of this book includes some historical perspectives on the computational revolution that laid a foundation for the explosion of machine learning and AI research and applications. The new transdiscipline of DSS is more focused on addressing societal problems with data and systems. When I look back across the seven decades that preceded the founding of IDSS, I see a handful of key developments and entities that set the stage for our new transdiscipline at MIT. Those developments comprise evolutions in system theory, information and decision sciences, social and economic networks, and econometrics. In many respects, one might aptly dub DSS as "Cybernetics 2.0." What sets this approach apart is its innovative integration of systems thinking into the realm of data and information, forging a unified methodology to effectively tackle intricate societal challenges.

1940s–1950s	Servomechanism Lab established at MIT featuring the Aircraft Stability Analyzer and Whirlwind project that developed the first high-speed computer, headed by J.W. Forrester, who is credited with perfecting magnetic core-memory, the forerunner to today's random-access memory (RAM). Forrester also founded the field of system dynamics, which integrates social dynamics with engineered systems. Claude E. Shannon introduced information theory in his 1949 book *A Mathematical Theory of Communication*, which had a profound impact on communication systems and statistics. Weiner summarized his work in *Cybernetics* that became the genesis of system theory and feedback as a way of modeling all kinds of interactions ranging from technical and biological to social.
1960s	Modern control theory advanced by a core group of faculty members in MIT's Engineering Systems Laboratory (ESL)) – an evolution of the Servomechanism Lab – in such key publications as "Analytical Design of Linear Feedback Controls" (G. C. Newton, L. A. Gould, and J. F. Kaiser) and *Optimal Control: An Introduction to the Theory and Its Applications* (M. Athans and P. L. Falb). Robert

G. Gallager contributed to the evolution of coding theory with the invention of low-density parity-check (LDPC) codes in 1963, but it would be 30 years before LDPC codes would be applied directly in computing.

1974   Herman Chernoff joins the MIT Mathematics Department to build a statistics presence at the Institute. He subsequently left MIT in 1985 without much success in launching a statistics effort.

1978   ESL evolves into the Laboratory for Information and Decision Systems (LIDS), expanding its scope to address a broader range of problems requiring the methods and perspectives of information, decision, and control and generating key publications such as *Data Networks* (D. P. Bertsekas and R. G. Gallager).

1970s–1980s   Jerry Hausman, Frank Fisher, and Dan McFadden helped to establish the foundations of modern econometric analysis. Each published important work that shaped the field, including McFadden's "Conditional Logit Analysis of Qualitative Choice Behavior" on discrete choice models and Hausman's "Specification Tests in Econometrics" on specification analysis. During this period, MIT launched its Technology and Policy Program to address the challenging policy questions emerging from new technologies.

1980s–2000s   Robust control theory, intelligent control systems, and distributed computation were developed and supported by the publication of *Parallel and Distributed Computation* (D. P. Bertsekas and J.N. Tsitsiklis). Computational approaches to control and reinforcement learning developed and represented in such publications as *Neurodynamic Programming* (D. P. Bertsekas and J.N. Tsitsiklis) and *Control of Uncertain Systems: A Linear Programming Approach* (M. A. Dahleh and I. Diaz-Bobillo).

2000s   New foundations laid in convex and non-convex analysis put forward in *Sum of Squares: Theory and Applications* (P. A. Parrilo and R. R. Thomas), inference, ML, and graphical methods found in *Gossip Algorithms* (D. Shah).

2010s   Physical, economic, and social networks have become important areas of academic research and problem-solving. "Systemic Risk and Stability in Financial Networks" and other work by Daron Acemoglu, Asu Ozdaglar, and Alireza Tahbaz-Salehi contributed greatly to the areas of network economics, cascades, and systemic risk. Alex "Sandy" Pentland's *Social Physics* pushed the boundaries of our understanding of the underpinnings of social interconnections.

2015   MIT launched IDSS to integrate the Institute's broader activities in science, technology, humanities, arts, and social sciences with data-driven research aimed at solving various societal challenges. IDSS integrated multiple developments in statistics, information, and decision sciences to define the fundamental principles for data-driven research addressing societal problems.

2019   MIT established the Schwarzman College of Computing to strengthen computing studies and research across all disciplines.

With this rich legacy encompassing systems theory, information theory, social and economic networks, econometrics, and cybernetics, the IDSS transdisciplinary approach converges at the crossroads of these domains. Such developments laid the groundwork for interactions among physical, social, and institutional systems that formed the foundation of our triangle.

The New Statistics

Given the vibrancy of information and decision sciences at MIT, we turned our attention to statistics. As noted earlier in the timeline at the beginning of this chapter, Chernoff came to MIT to launch an effort in statistics. Unfortunately, that effort failed and Chernoff departed for Harvard. The timeline also highlights that econometrics continued to thrive at MIT, despite the absence of a central statistics effort. Given the fact that MIT always has been a strong engineering institution, statistics and data-driven thinking already were present in almost every discipline. The Department of Economics, as well, pushed for laying the foundations of econometrics early on. As a result, no one unit could claim ownership of this important field.

This was evident in the many courses offered by multiple academic units at MIT, each addressing statistics from the perspective of its own domain. What we lost with this approach was the opportunity of having such efforts collide and interact both in education and research. Given the critical role data played in the IDSS vision, our response was to create the Statistics and Data Science Center (SDSC) to focus on the educational needs of a new kind of statistics that was emerging. A key innovation of the center was to create an option for statistics not to reside in any single unit within MIT (a solution for which MIT lacked an aptitude). At long last, we had a cohesive statistics effort at MIT that could operate at the intersection of all domains.

SDSC provided the platform we needed to develop and teach new, twenty-first-century statistics suited to the issues and methods associated with big data: large, noisy, and unlabeled data sets; high dimensional, noisy, and possibly sparse data; multiscale, time-varying data sets; rare and highly aggregated data; and intervention and experimental design. All those issues come into play when we attempt to solve complex societal problems using machine-learning tools and algorithmic and optimization methods. The new statistics enable us to assess the accuracy and robustness of our models and to distinguish between causality and correlation.

Building Bridges between Computational and Social Sciences

In so far as statistics, information, and decision systems played pivotal roles in shaping the new transdisciplinary approach of IDSS, so did the domains of social sciences and humanities with their focus on social and institutional behavior. The timeline presented earlier in this chapter notes the seminal work of Forrester and Weiner in bringing systems theory and feedback to the analysis of social systems. With the incorporation of rich data sets going forward, the opportunity is even greater.

First and foremost, IDSS needed to attract computational social scientists among our existing faculty to serve as the bridge between engineers, scientists, computer scientists, and social scientists and humanists. In the design of a new doctoral program, the participation of a co-advisor from the social sciences was essential to ensure that students framed their inquiries to include perspectives extending beyond purely technical considerations. IDSS faced the challenge of devising methods to encourage and facilitate such interdisciplinary collaborations while dismantling the natural barriers that arise from distinct research approaches. More on that point further on in this book.

The Rationale for Integrating Domain Knowledge

Starting in 2015 and continuing into the 2020s, we at IDSS have been intensely focused on how best to prepare the future data-science learner. A distinctly MIT aspect of our efforts has been the focus on systems in addition to data. Sustained and dynamic inquiries into systems design and architecture that explain the data generation and support modeling and prediction of system behaviors and performance are a hallmark of IDSS activities. We believe that a systems-based methodology – well integrated with domain knowledge – is essential to the success of data science initiatives intent on delivering societal benefits.

As ML became an accessible and standard research tool, however, many proponents of the technology wandered unbeknownst into a danger zone. ML was, and still is, being applied to societal problems without consideration for particular domain knowledge that may be essential to understanding a complex system's design, behaviors, and performance. Domains such as sociology and economics, for instance, achieved disciplinary status before the advent of data science, and much of the knowledge and practices of those disciplines are foreign to contemporary data scientists.

Data science is most effective when it is fully integrated with domain expertise and vice versa. Experts in biology, urban planning, supply chains, chemical processes, pollution, or gender bias, for example, must be equipped with a rigorous understanding of data science and computational thinking to ensure a systematic approach to research and problem-solving. In the context of our earlier discussion about racial bias in Chapter 3, it's no wonder that combating systemic racism has captured the attention of data scientists – and inspired a specific initiative within IDSS (more on that project a little later in this chapter). Effective research in this area certainly explores and collects relevant data across multiple domains in which racism has been – and continues to be – prominent.

Unfortunately, such research can lead to erroneous conclusions and self-fulfilling cycles of inequities if it does not pay full attention to how data are collected. Specific domain expertise is needed to identify explicit and implicit ways that racial bias may seep into data collection processes. Quantifying the uncertainty of results using data science also plays a critical role here, as it does in the development of algorithmic solutions in any domain. Assessing the reliability of our results must be integrated into the implementation of our recommendations. Failing to do so risks grave, regrettable, and potentially avoidable mistakes that can cause personal harm or weaken society. One can project all of these issues to the algorithmic bias created in the approval of loan applications to see the degree of damage data science can create. The work of MIT MLK Professor Craig Watkins on facial recognition tools (described in Chapter 3) is another example of this destructive phenomenon.

Translating the IDSS Triangle into a Flagship Academic Program

Having established some fundamental objectives and identified a number of cautions, the founders of IDSS faced the practical challenge of creating curricula that would be compelling to students and faculty members – and be intelligible to the world outside MIT. The IDSS signature PhD program, Social and Engineering Systems (SES), emerged from those efforts.

Societal challenges, by their very nature, involve intensive data about human activities (individual and institutional) as well as systems that govern mechanisms for generating data and experimentation such as engineering, economic, or financial systems. We designed SES to include core competencies and training necessary to tackle such challenges. It set the standard for rigorous analysis of those challenges and created a common language for productive interactions among all relevant domains.

The SES curriculum comprises the elements of the IDSS Triangle (systems, human and social interactions, and institutional interactions) on a foundation of three educational pillars:

- information sciences (probabilistic modeling, information theory, optimization, and decision theory);

- twenty-first century statistics (more on that later in this chapter);
- humanities and social science studies.

SES doctoral students acquire in-depth expertise in all three pillars as they study one or more particular domains (e.g., energy systems, finance, healthcare, social networks, urban systems, misinformation, democracy, racism). The overall framework enables students to address questions related to assessment, design, and ethics. It also enables our graduates to pursue foundational research and knowledge discovery in their particular domains and makes them distinctly powerful problem-solvers in organizations seeking to solve complex societal challenges.

For individuals with backgrounds in the computational and model-driven fields of engineering and computing, those first two pillars will seem quite natural. Traditional statistics involves mapping data to probabilistic models that researchers and decision-makers can use for prediction, intervention, and assessment. The third pillar, however, introduces conceptual frameworks and research methods from the social sciences and humanities that historically haven't been incorporated into computational modeling, such as collective/organizational behavior and ethical guidelines.

SES PhD theses typically are problem-driven, so expertise in the domain most closely related to the problem is essential. Without such knowledge, abstractions may miss critical aspects of the challenge veer toward meaninglessness. The core curriculum – and the mandatory PhD seminar, in particular – teaches students how to formulate questions and create abstractions that offer multiple views of a single problem or set of closely related problems within any domain. Finally, the program creates and sustains a culture of common tools and knowledge that facilitates interactions among a variety of researchers across multiple domains, which is why we consider SES to be the flagship program of IDSS.

Statistics and Data Science: Residential and Online Education

To teach the new statistics within IDSS, we launched the Interdisciplinary Doctoral Program in Statistics (IDPS) as well as an undergraduate minor and the online MicroMaster's in Statistics and Data Science. As a group, these three programs ensure that MIT students at all levels – and from every department – have the opportunity to develop an advanced understanding of twenty-first century statistics and data science. The curricula comprise concepts of probabilistic modeling, statistics, computation, and data analysis within each student's chosen field of study. Many MIT programs from each of the Institute's five schools have engaged with the IDPS program.

The Statistics and Data Science MicroMasters (SDS) online program, launched in 2018, gives remote learners around the world the opportunity to earn professional and academic credentials applicable to a variety of fields. Global demand for data scientists is high, and the field is growing rapidly. SDS helps fulfill the need for transdisciplinary capabilities by providing both foundational knowledge and hands-on experience in statistics and data science. This online program can be applied to residential programs at more than 25 pathway universities. Those partnerships enable students to obtain high-quality advanced degrees more efficiently and at less cost than traditional programs.

The online (synchronous and asynchronous) format of this program also enables us to customize the offering to the needs of any partner institution. Our flagship collaboration with Aporta, a social impact lab founded in Peru by the business conglomerate Breca, has led us to multiple other collaborations across the world. Within Aporta, Briet (Brescia Institute of Technology) is a social impact lab founded by Ana Maria Brescia Cafferata (co-owner of the Breca Group) in 2018 to promote societal development. The IDSS component focuses on creating the next generation of data scientists among Peruvian nationals. The program combines hands-on technical training with soft-skills development in leadership and teamwork. The Peruvian students also participate regularly in MIT online events and initiatives such as ISOLAT, MIT's data-driven global response to the COVID-19 pandemic.

IDSS's dedication to online education aligns with the growing societal focus on the importance of learning opportunities. The demand for education in data science is not only widespread globally but also essential at the professional level. Alongside the MicroMasters, IDSS and its faculty have developed various online programs to provide professional education in Data Science, Machine Learning, and Artificial Intelligence to learners worldwide. These programs adhere to a principled approach that is consistent with IDSS's overarching value proposition.

Technology Policy Program

At the professional level, IDSS hosts the Master of Science in Technology and Policy Program (TPP), which first launched at MIT in 1976. TPP's mission is to develop leaders who can create, refine, implement, and evaluate responsible policies informed by an understanding of technology and its instruments, as well as the broad social contexts in which those tools are deployed. By combining a core of science and engineering study with applied social sciences, TPP students develop strengths in both a technical field (e.g., telecom networks, energy, transportation, healthcare, the environment) and policy processes. With the emersion in IDSS, TPP supports data-driven policy research (both evaluation and experimental analysis) and addresses important policy issues with data privacy and ethical consideration. The program complements the other existing academic programs.

The Human Architecture of a New Transdiscipline

The particulars of how we built the new academic unit of IDSS likely are relevant to existing and future initiatives at other institutions. More useful still, I think, are the underlying principles that informed the choices we made. We used the vision of the IDSS Triangle (discussed in detail in Chapter 4) as a means of thinking about complex, multidimensional problems in a variety of specific domains. That vision required us to apply statistical and systems thinking as frameworks for making decisions under uncertainty as well as to convene and sustain a new mix of people who could bring our vision to life.

The committee responsible for shaping IDSS at its inception proposed that this novel entity be designated an Institute at MIT. In the context of MIT, an Institute is akin to a department, the distinction being the composition of its faculty. Faculty members at an MIT Institute can hail from various departments and hold joint positions within MIT, resulting in a unique cross-disciplinary dynamic. Given the expansive scope of IDSS, faculty could belong to any department among MIT's five schools. When it was established, therefore, IDSS reported to all the deans of the five schools. That changed in 2019 when IDSS became part of the newly formed Schwarzman College of Computing. As one of the objectives of the new college was to bring computing to various domains, it became clear that IDSS – with an aligned, yet more specific, vision – should become an independent unit within the college.

The organizational structure of a new academic entity is crucial to the realization of its vision, and universities can struggle to accommodate nontraditional structures while fostering the growth into interdisciplinary education and research. From our perspective, IDSS's role was to infuse a transdisciplinary ethos into diverse disciplines. The structural framework we chose was designed to incentivize all participating departments to actively contribute to IDSS's success, in large part because their faculty held joint appointments in our Institute. That arrangement was often likened to reverse ownership, and it gave each department a stake in IDSS's accomplishments.

Faculty Hiring

On the faculty side, we sought a range of experts related to statistics – theoretical and applied. Such candidates' expertise might overlap with information and decision sciences (i.e., interconnections, networks, feedback, optimization) – as well as specific domains with a particular focus on the social sciences. Our goal was to create a vibrant, multidimensional educational effort in statistics that would attract students who were eager to focus their master's or doctoral work on solving complex societal problems. In addition, those students needed sustained access to a variety of domain experts (e.g., faculty members in environmental science, economics, political science, management, etc.).

Given those objectives, we knew that launching IDSS as traditional academic department – which typically organizes around a core set of courses, topics, research areas, and faculty members – would hinder our objective of intersecting with many, or all, existing MIT departments. We also had no interest in dictating to any existing department what they should teach its students within its domain. Instead, we wanted to infuse our new statistical, information-systems, and decision-systems thinking and methodologies within each department interested in engaging with IDSS. We wanted to build a transdiscipline that could build bridges among disciplines and enable each department to take ownership of the development of our transdiscipline within their respective domains.

With those transdisciplinary organizing principles to guide us, we used a nontraditional approach for faculty hiring and student recruitment. The last thing we wanted was to disconnect existing faculty members from their departments, or worse, bring in new faculty members who lacked strong departmental ties to existing domains at MIT. The approach we adopted – which persists to this day – was to comprise a faculty of core members who belonged partially to IDSS and partially to their home departments. They agreed to divide their teaching and administrative responsibilities equally between both entities and to work with students who integrated the data and systems aspects of IDSS with the problems and methods of the applicable domains.

Rather than redirect, distract, or otherwise derail any faculty members from domain-specific research and teaching, our model helped boost the reach and rigor of disciplinary work. The presence of IDSS faculty members with core competencies in statistics, data science, information systems, decision science, and social sciences ensured access to the foundational education and research activities that experts in other disciplines could utilize and adapt within their domains.

That opportunity was easy to sell to tenured MIT professors in established departments, but it presented potential complications for junior faculty members and non-tenured new hires. The risk, at least initially, was that dividing their time between their home departments and IDSS would be perceived as a distraction from research, teaching, and home-department responsibilities that pave the path to tenure. To avoid that pitfall, senior IDSS faculty placed special emphasis on mentoring junior colleagues in applying IDSS resources to pioneering research within their home domains. MIT as a whole also played an important role in the early years by helping to fund novel research empowered by our new transdiscipline until it became institutionalized within each domain. At the end, the interaction between IDSS and various departments gave a huge advantage to the newly hired junior faculty.

IDSS bears a significant responsibility to assist departments in building capacity within the emerging transdiscipline of data, systems, and society (DSS), especially through faculty recruitment. Those efforts include jointly managed search committees that identify and attract the right candidates. Although each department may have a distinct approach to recruitment, the involvement of IDSS ensures that all candidates are aligned with the intended vision for the respective positions. While that process poses challenges, it also promotes an understanding within MIT departments of the role and competency of recruited faculty.

Nurturing the Trilingual Student

In conceiving academic programs for IDSS, we were very deliberate about nurturing trilingual students. In addition to being experts in statistics and information sciences, those individuals also would need to possess a deep understanding of social and institutional behavior alongside expertise in their chosen research domains. Our recruitment process extended beyond consideration of mere academic excellence. We identified students who were determined to transcend traditional disciplinary boundaries to focus on addressing pressing societal challenges. The students who joined IDSS embodied an entrepreneurial spirit that facilitated their navigation of intricate domains, the forging of valuable collaborations and, ultimately, the realization of the IDSS vision. Our experience shows that such students exhibit remarkable versatility, effortlessly traversing various domains thanks to their exceptional competence in statistics, information science, and the foundational aspects of social and institutional studies.

Collaboration among our students across various MIT units is key to the success of our educational and research programs. The concept of research groups – colleagues working collaboratively on shared objectives with students and postdocs – is very common among, engineers and computer scientists. That approach – which is a critical component of IDSS programs – is much less common in the social sciences and humanities. At IDSS, we took on the significant task of bridging such gaps between academic communities by addressing financial dependencies and nurturing a culture of engagement that encourages individuals to step outside their comfort zones and work collaboratively.

The distinct nature of SES, in which students are supervised by multiple faculty (with a strong emphasis on humanities and social sciences), inspired us to dedicate financial resources to support student research. The overarching objective is to provide equitable support for students to freely explore open-ended societal problems. IDSS plays a crucial role as an enabler of new research, by providing essential resources for lines of inquiry that may not align with conventional research in specific disciplines or domains. Over time, our transdisciplinary approach has become institutionalized, and our researchers are finding it easier to secure independent funding for their projects.

IDSS also enhances capacity through postdoctoral fellows who work at the intersection of this emerging transdiscipline and numerous specific domains. IDSS fellows collaborate directly with faculty members from various fields across campus as well as their respective students.

Professional Considerations in the Wider World

In tandem with figuring out how the mindset and methods of our transdiscipline flow into traditional domains, we had to factor in publishing options for core IDSS faculty as well as potential job prospects for IDSS graduates. The importance of publications to an academic career arc is well established – both the quality of one's academic papers and the prestige of the journals in which they appear are pivotal. In the early years, becoming members of the DSS transdiscipline required our faculty to continue publishing in domain-specific journals while at the same time infusing the statistical, information systems, and decision systems into their overall approaches. Over time, we also expect to see and support the rise of more transdisciplinary-centric journals that welcome submissions from a wide range of domains (*Harvard Data Science Review*, launched in 2019, is an early example of such publications).

Our early emphasis on high-quality, domain-specific publications was essential for our graduate students. Many published their transdisciplinary work in well-respected disciplinary journals and launched their scholarly careers at academic institutions with comparable rigor to MIT. Progressing from master's and doctoral studies into private sector jobs was never a problem for our graduates. Business and industry have always been much less siloed than academia, and the transdisciplinary capabilities of IDSS alumni enable them to formulate and solve complex, dynamic problems with entirely new tools –including those that have yet to be invented.

Academic job placements also can be challenging to secure without successful discipline-specific publications. At IDSS, we're helping students bridge that gap by actively engaging with established disciplinary fields to which our students contribute.

Physical Space Is Critical

The IDSS space has been crucial for fostering collaboration and innovation within our academic institution. Our senior administrative team recognized that physical space for IDSS – a truly scarce resource at MIT – would be crucial to achieving our stated mission. The IDSS space accommodates students, postdocs, and faculty in shared offices (a configuration that has turned out to be both sufficient and preferred by the occupants).

The space has allowed for spontaneous interactions and random encounters that facilitate learning about each other's work – a phenomenon that is difficult to replicate virtually. The physical interaction has been particularly effective in enabling students to learn from both their peers and faculty members. The IDSS space also provides a venue for events, seminars, and social gatherings and houses capabilities such as a visualization lab. Overall, the space serves as a welcoming hub for researchers to explore collaboration opportunities and expand the interdisciplinary nature of our work.

Initiative on Combatting Systemic Racism: Case in Point

Racism is one of America's most enduring and formidable existential challenges. Researchers have illuminated racial discrimination across various facets of society – labor market, the criminal justice system, education, healthcare, housing access, financial services, and many others. At several earlier points in this book, we've addressed the critical issue of systemic bias and its intricate relationship with the fields of computing and data science. When we address systemic racism, our focus is not on individual prejudice but rather on the systems in place that inadvertently exacerbate biases against Blacks, Latinos, and other historically underserved communities. Those systems may not harbor explicit intentions to perpetuate such biases, but the unintended consequences do so, nonetheless. As we have illustrated in earlier chapters, computation and data have played a significant role in amplifying the effects of racism in areas ranging from the US Census, policing, and surveillance to climate justice, credit scoring, and healthcare.

When my colleague Fotini Christia and I launched the Initiative on Combatting Systemic Racism in 2021, we recognized that IDSS provided the ideal platform for this complex endeavor. By definition, DSS is a transdisciplinary field that serves as the foundational methodology for addressing challenges that span multiple institutional and policy domains. We also discerned the intricate interplay among various domains such as housing and healthcare are inextricably intertwined in their impact on Black communities in the US

IDSS is exceptionally well-positioned to foster collaboration among faculty members from diverse disciplines who can help address this challenge. We've leveraged the extensive body of literature within the social sciences and forged partnerships across the technical fields of data science and computing to tackle the issues highlighted by our social science colleagues. Our transdisciplinary team has developed concept papers that serve as cornerstones for broader collaboration among our faculty, and we've included a few examples of that work in the following sections.

Translating Analysis into Action

Beyond elucidating the problem, our mission includes developing proactive policy solutions to rectify racially inequitable outcomes stemming from implicit or explicit biases entrenched in institutional practices of both public and private sectors. We've expanded our work to confront the evolving challenges introduced by the utilization of AI and algorithmic methods in decision-making that exacerbate this complex problem.

Our research collects and delves into vast data sets spanning numerous domains. We meticulously examine data-collection processes to pinpoint explicit or implicit sources of racial bias. We're using those insights to develop and enhance data-driven computational tools engineered that address racial disparities within the structures and institutions that perpetuate discriminatory outcomes in the US economy and broader society. Because the work is deeply rooted in ethical and societal considerations, we're firmly committed to coordinating and sharing our findings with local stakeholders from historically disadvantaged groups as well as to driving relevant policy decisions that will contribute to a more equitable society.

IDSS students and postdocs are greatly inspired by and engaged with this initiative. In the work, they face complex technical challenges that demand sensitive and socially conscious solutions. They're delving into problems ranging from the robust debiasing of data to the delicate task of eliminating racial indicators without compromising valuable societal information. They're also scrutinizing the persistence of historical patterns of segregation that continue to influence contemporary processes. As an academic framework, the SES program has provided the ideal preparation for students eager to apply the DSS transdisciplinary approach to address persistent societal challenges. Our research community naturally fosters transdisciplinary synergy and facilitates the convergence of collaborators across diverse domains.

Outreach and Engagement

In seeking to combat systemic racism, IDSS has opened its doors for outreach and engagement with historically underserved communities in both education and research endeavors. Leveraging the Minority Summer Research Program (MSRP) at MIT, IDSS hosted a cohort of students with a keen interest in conducting research in this area. We welcomed those budding researchers by embracing their distinct life experiences and acknowledging their individual contributions. Our core goals for the program were beautifully expressed in MSRP student Savannah Gregory's reflection, "I feel confident that I am viewed as an extension of the team, a member whose perspective is valued. As I reflect on my experiences, I now see MIT and IDSS as environments where intellect is nurtured and curiosity is actively encouraged."

IDSS also has extended its online educational programs to benefit many students in historically Black colleges and universities (HBCUs), offering them opportunities to delve deeper into the realm of data science and its practical applications. Working with MIT Professional Education and its partner Great Learning, we adapted the highly successful Machine Learning and Data Science online course for a summer program tailored to underserved students. We provided the course free of charge and paired cohorts of students with MIT doctoral teaching assistants who introduced students through this rapidly evolving field. We expect the initiative to play a crucial role in developing the pipeline of students interested in this domain.

A Deep Dive into Systemic Racism and Policing

My IDSS colleagues have undertaken diverse inquiries related to systemic racism, including an examination of the root causes of confrontations between the police and potential suspects. While the media often emphasizes prejudice in interactions among police and individuals of color, the work of IDSS faculty and students interrogates additional contributing factors. We've learned, for example, that many police-citizen interactions stem from 911 calls, prompting researchers to query the possibility that biases embedded in those calls may influence subsequent police behavior – and create a cascade of racist actions.

After analyzing a vast data set comprising more than 22 million 911 records and 400,000+ police stops, my IDSS colleagues Fotini Christia, Devavrat Shah, Craig Watkins, and their SES students discovered that calls related to people of color are more likely to result in police actions versus reports involving White citizens. In their 2024 paper "A causal framework to evaluate racial bias in law enforcement system," the researchers investigated the sources of bias in various scenarios including airport security, AI-driven security, and encounters resulting from 911 calls. In the future, they hope to extend their study to examine the content and sentiment of 911 calls to determine if they have a causal impact on police actions that goes beyond simply over-reporting. The research framework – built on extensive data and sophisticated modeling that integrates disparate data sets – offers a robust approach to comprehending aspects of the justice system marred by a cascade of biased activities.

Housing and Eviction Disparities

Recent scholarly discourse conducted by my colleague Peko Hosio and her SES student Aurora Zhang related to housing has shed light on the intricate and compelling relationship between neighborhood racial composition and eviction rates. Drawing from the rich tapestry of the Eviction Lab data set, a rigorous exploration revealed a pronounced and persistent correlation between neighborhood racial composition and eviction rates – even after meticulous adjustments for economic variables such as poverty rate, median income, and median rent.

In the course of this academic pursuit, Two pivotal inquiries have emerged from this academic research. The first looks at the concealed mechanisms underlying the integration of racial disparities into the fabric of eviction. The second investigates whether the application of causal inference methods can illuminate the study of policies designed to disentangle and alleviate these disparities. The unfolding discourse on these topics is poised to uncover layers of understanding and potential responses to the nuanced interplay of neighborhood demographics and fluctuating patterns of eviction.

Discriminatory Online Content and Actions

As of the writing of this book, my colleagues are immersed in a fascinating investigation that seeks to comprehend the relationship between bias in social media and offline discriminatory behavior. Numerous studies have already revealed that discriminatory content online can translate into harmful real-world actions. Researchers are delving into questions of how the depiction of various demographic groups correlates with specific instances of offline discrimination. The research seeks to establish whether individuals' identities and attributes play a role in shaping the connection between online content consumption and subsequent offline behavior. Taken as a whole, this growing body of work continues to uncover systemic racism in multiple domains ranging from healthcare and policing to housing, social media, and climate change.

7 PEOPLE, PROGRAMS, AND RESEARCH
Perpetuating a Virtuous Cycle

As I ruminate on what coalesced at IDSS during the nine years after we formally launched in 2015, I risk giving the impression that we began with a fully formed sense of what we wanted the culture of our new discipline to be. In truth, we didn't spend much time talking about our vision for the culture at the outset. Instead, we focused on what we believed to be the necessary ingredients for tackling the interdisciplinary challenges arising from complex societal and technical systems. Those ingredients included statistics, stochastic modeling, information theory and inference, systems and control theory, optimization, economics, network science, and human and social behavior. We also were particularly attentive to community-building at IDSS. We recognized from the start that our main purpose was to create a new culture around a new transdiscipline.

We were confident that the collision and synthesis of ideas and methods from these analytical disciplines would produce a distinct and fertile environment for transformative research. We also understood that our vision depended heavily on attracting like-minded research and teaching colleagues as well as a species of graduate students that we couldn't be sure existed. We believed that we could build it, but would they come? If they came, we wanted the culture of our new discipline to grow up among us out of the community we formed together. We remained attentive to community-building by reminding one another that it's much easier to launch programs than it is to build a culture.

The PhDs Will Lead Us

As the birthplace of IDSS, MIT – with its motto "mens et manus" (mind and hand) – had much to recommend it. Problem-solving is an essential element of the Institute's DNA, as is the passion of its faculty and researchers for breaking new ground and collaborating across traditional disciplinary boundaries. All the resources, talent, experience, and inspiration of MIT were necessary – but not sufficient – conditions for IDSS to thrive. Ultimately, the new institute needed to attract, educate, and retain a new breed of doctoral students who could bring creativity, entrepreneurial spirit, and enthusiasm for the experimental to their work. (Refer back to Chapter 6 for an overview of the design of such PhD programs.) Our hope was to show the world the full significance of MIT's motto through the embodiment of its third, unspoken component – heart – which energizes the humanistic approach to problem-solving that IDSS was championing.

Most of all, our new IDSS PhD students need to possess a preternatural facility to work expertly and fluidly among multiple disciplines including statistics, information sciences, engineering, and social sciences. In conjunction with those skill sets, IDSS students had to master a real-world domain such as media, transportation, or energy markets. Even as they pioneered this powerful combination of capabilities, these doctoral students would establish the foundation of a new teaching and research community. They would be central to the propagation of the IDSS culture and would energize and broaden the faculty who contributed to this new discipline.

Extracting Data-Driven Environmental Policies from the "Beijing Haze"

"Imagine waking up at 8:00am and thinking it's 8:00pm because it's so dark." That's how IDSS SES doctoral student Minghao Qiu – who arrived at MIT in 2016 – recounts his personal experience of the Beijing Haze during the winter of 2013. Researchers quantified the human cost of that catastrophic air-pollution phenomenon to include hundreds of premature deaths and tens of thousands of acute bronchitis and asthma cases. The same research team estimated the related economic losses to be in excess of $250 million.

For Qiu, the Haze was galvanizing. He resolved to shine a light on a more complicated aspect of the crisis by studying air pollution, energy, and public policy as a complex system that produced multiple undesirable outcomes. To do that, Qiu needed the support of a research community distinctly focused on tackling broad societal challenges using rigorous data analysis. Qiu brought to IDSS his Peking University training in economics and environmental science, and his SES program colleagues helped him understand how climate-related issues interact with other components of human society.

In his first research 2020 paper at MIT (published by *Environmental Science & Technology* in 2020), Qiu collaborated with his IDSS research advisor, Professor Noelle Selin and colleagues from Tsinghua and Carnegie Mellon universities to develop a rare "ex-post" (retrospective) analysis of the policies that may have contributed to the Beijing Haze of 2013. A key objective of the team was to demonstrate how retrospective analyses of past policies could improve projections about the consequences of a potential new policy during its formative stage. The study manifested a core objective that Qiu shared in common with the entire IDSS community – demonstrating how data can be used to address a wide range of complex societal problems.

Qiu characterized his experience of the IDSS culture in a conversation with *MIT News* in 2018. "IDSS/SES's focus on data-driven policy studies is a perfect fit with my research interest, and I really enjoy the interdisciplinary atmosphere ... IDSS/SES allows me to gain a solid training on both quantitative methods and social sciences. I also value the opportunity to work with my two co-advisors very closely, which motivates my research from both science and policy perspectives. The interactions with students and faculty from different backgrounds helps me to reflect on my own research from different perspectives. Although we focus on different problems, my cohorts' perspectives greatly enhance my thinking about quantitative methods and research design."

Measuring Distrust Born of Clickbait

PhD student Manon Revel grew up in the suburbs of Paris, France, with a passion for journalism – her father's profession. As a teenager, she reported for the local radio station and launched a school newspaper. When Revel had to choose a field of study at university, however, she picked science. She earned bachelor's and master's degrees in engineering and applied mathematics at École Centrale Paris while continuing to work as a journalist in her spare time.

As she contemplated her next move, Revel looked for opportunities that would unite her varied interests. "I always felt like I had these different lives," Revel told *MIT News* in 2020. "Coming to MIT was the first time I felt that my interests could finally be put together, and that I could work on everything in unison." Her plan was for a second master's degree only, but she found the transdisciplinary ecosystem emerging within IDSS compelling. She joined the SES doctoral program in 2017 and set to work analyzing the turbulent dynamics of journalism and society in the aftermath of the 2016 US presidential election.

With advisors from four academic domains – civil and environmental engineering, management, political science, and electrical engineering and computer science – Revel teamed up with Amir Tohidi, a graduate student in the LIDS, to study the effects of clickbait ads on reader trust. This formulation is an indication of the thoughtful thinking around such issues in IDSS – in contrast to much of the work that was done that focused on detecting such clickbait. For their research, Revel and her colleagues defined clickbait as a headline or other concise text designed to trigger clicks on a hyperlink that leads to content of dubious value or interest. The team trained AI – a Bayesian text classification program, in this instance – to recognize clickbait and put the tool to work analyzing nearly 1.5 million online ads from 2016 to 2019.

Revel's data scrap revealed that more than 80% of the ads were clickbait. Subsequent large-scale and carefully designed randomized experiments showed that a single exposure to clickbait in proximity to legitimate content undermined readers' confidence in that content and in the publication as a whole. The effect was most notable for publications with medium familiarity – that is, recognition among 25% to 50% of the audience. Among widely recognized sources such as *CNN* and *Fox News*, however, the effect was negligible. In a time of rampant information disorder, Revel hopes these findings will encourage journalism publishers to think twice before chasing the short-term profits associated with clickbait at the expense of readers' fundamental trust in their reporting. She also seeks to expand this line of research to examine questions such as how people process information related to their voting decisions, including in her 2021 paper "Native advertising and the credibility of online publishers" with collaborators Amir Tohidi, Dean Eckles, and Adam Berinsky.

IDSS Faculty Are Strong Attractors

During the first eight years of its existence, the IDSS student cohort grew rapidly – doctoral, master's, and other MIT students affiliated with IDSS through their advisors. In 2022, our students' backgrounds spanned the disciplines of engineering, political science, economics, management, statistics, and mathematics. This diverse cohort was the product of a virtuous cycle that originated with IDSS faculty recruitment.

As explained in Chapter 6, our initial hiring strategy was based on two key objectives – broaden domain engagement internally and expand our statistics firepower with new faculty. To diversify internal engagement, we welcomed faculty hires and affiliates from within all five of MIT's schools and a remarkably diverse group of departments: Anthropology, Comparative Media Studies, Media Lab, Information Technology, Organization Studies, Management Studies, Urban Studies and Planning, Political Science, Economics, Mathematics, Physics, Brain and Cognitive Sciences, Electrical Engineering and Computer Science, Civil and Environmental Engineering, and Mechanical Engineering.

To grow MIT's statistics capabilities, we recruited external candidates with nontraditional perspectives in key subject areas such as information theory, high-dimensional and online learning, theoretical computer science, optimization, econometrics, and networks as well as core statistics. By 2022, we had developed a large and diverse roster of joint faculty and affiliate members.

Intersectional Research Leads to Actionable Breakthroughs

Associate Professor Caroline Uhler, who came to MIT in 2015 with joint appointments in IDSS and Electrical Engineering and Computer Science (EECS), exemplifies the qualities that make the IDSS faculty cohort so compelling to our students. Uhler combines deep research expertise with broad vision, strong leadership skills, and a passion for teaching. In fact, she graduated from high school in Switzerland with a plan to teach math, biology, and languages at the secondary level.

All that changed when Uhler encountered algebraic statistics for computational biology in graduate school. She changed course and headed to UC Berkeley for a PhD in statistics. Although much of her early work was theoretical, her fascination with the nexus of biology and math (in this case, algebra and statistics) led her to study causality and gene regulation as a means of learning more about what's going on inside a cell.

At MIT, Uhler's work expanded to incorporate ML tools alongside methods from statistics and biology. This approach enabled her to integrate and translate among vastly different existing data models used in the study of single-cell biology. One particularly promising application of that work was to reveal how a particular disease impacts the body at a cellular level, which in turn could result in more targeted treatments for a variety of maladies.

In 2021, the same year Uhler was named co-director of the Eric and Wendy Schmidt Center at the Broad Institute of MIT and Harvard, her research group co-authored a paper that applied these new techniques to the global pandemic. The approach identified existing drugs that could be repurposed to fight COVID-19. In addition to helping pinpoint drug candidates for clinical trials, the team's research can be applied to other diseases where detailed gene-expression data exist.

ML-Aided Cancer Research

Uhler's application of statistics and ML to genomic research has expanded to include cancer cells. In that pioneering work, her focus is on characterizing different types of cells – normal, fibrocystic, cancerous, and metastatic – using gene expression vectors of significant size (typically containing 20,000 elements). The objective is to identify which normal cells can transition into fibrocystic cells, which fibrocystic cells can become cancerous, and which cancer cells may become metastatic.

Several challenges complicate this investigation. The large size of a gene expression vector makes it difficult to pinpoint the subtle variations that lead to transitions between cell types. Representing genome expressions as vectors also can be limiting because the approach overlooks the underlying regulatory network structure that is critical to understanding how these expressions change. It's also problematic to track single cells through their evolution because most measurement techniques destroy the cells, which hinders traditional supervised learning algorithms.

To address those challenges, Uhler and her team are pursuing novel, ML-based approaches. Using nonlinear neural networks, auto-encoders perform principal-component reduction in high-dimensional genome expressions, which facilitates the detection of potential changes in expression. By utilizing optimal transport theory, the researchers are able to construct cell-to-cell mappings between categories based on their low-dimensional distributions. That approach provides the most efficient one-to-one association between two populations with a respective probability distribution that minimizes an expected cost function (which often is biologically motivated). Uhler and coauthor G. Shivashankar provide a good overview of this work in their 2022 article "Machine Learning Approaches to Single-Cell Data Integration and Translation."

The success of those ML-based tools inspired further research focused on intervention. Uhler's intervention program uses transcription factors (TFs) – cells with specific genome expressions that can bind with existing cells – to transform cell distributions. The goal is to discover an input-output function, which requires identification of the correct TFs from among millions of options. A key aspect of the research is to identify encoded variable-level structures that will simplify the search for new TFs from among previously explored options. This offers exciting opportunities for collaboration between control theory and genomics – additive or multiplicative structures, for example, can significantly reduce the search space.

Notwithstanding the technical complexity of Uhler's work, her efforts represent a signature aspect of the DSS transdiscipline that I hope nonexperts can appreciate – the productive and sustainable merging of network sciences, probability, causality, and low data structures to solve previously intractable problems. That, combined with the resolve of DSS to imbue such work with ethical guidelines and constraints, makes me very optimistic about the future.

The Holy Grail of Learning and Decisions

As a control theorist, I have long viewed every challenge as a decision problem. It was MIT Professor Emery Brown, however, who introduced me to the contemporary definition of statistics as "decisions under uncertainty." Initially, I found that statement perplexing. As time passed, though, I became convinced that Brown's perspective was the right approach to ML and statistics. Decisions under uncertainty are ubiquitous and lie at the core of the new statistical thinking.

Brown's anesthesia research exemplifies that mindset. Working with colleagues at MIT's Department of Brain and Cognitive Sciences, Brown used electroencephalogram (EEG) data to demonstrate that propofol – a common medication used for general anesthesia – significantly slows down brain dynamics, creating entirely new neurological patterns that differ significantly from those present during normal sleep. The common notion that patients are simply being "put to sleep" turns out to be highly misleading, and dispelling that myth has important implications for anesthesiologists and patients.

Although physicians and researchers have long observed that the administration of general anesthesia can contribute to brain dysfunction following surgery, they didn't understand the relevant mechanisms – or how to regulate them. Brown's research suggests that monitoring a patient's real-time EEG data during surgery could enable anesthesia equipment to administer drug levels more precisely and lower the risk of side effects. The approach uses a continuous feedback system that measures patient brain activity and adjusts medication levels accordingly. Brown and collaborators Patrick L. Purdon, Aaron Sampson, and Kara J. Pavone explore the topic in detail in their 2015 paper "Clinical Electroencephalography for Anesthesiologists Part I: Background and Basic Signatures."

To be successful, this approach must achieve a level of precision that adapts to individual patient variations and accurately detects a variety of brain states that potentially correlate with other vital signs routinely measured during surgery. The approach also poses a high-stakes fundamental research problem of integrating ML (on EEG data) and control systems (an anesthesia drip) in real-time. In control theory, we refer to such problems as safety critical because failure has extremely negative consequences. Brown's anesthesia research demonstrates that the complex, transdisciplinary interplay among ML tools, control systems, and patient safety is critical to the cutting-edge advances that will improve medical practice in the twenty-first century. It also represents yet another proof-of-concept for the habits of mind and methodologies of the new DSS discipline.

8 PERSONAL REFLECTIONS ON THE JOURNEY

I embarked on this endeavor not quite knowing what to expect. Although I had observed the launch of various initiatives and institutes at MIT (such as the Koch Institute for Integrative Cancer Research, Broad Institute, Institute for Medical Engineering and Science, and the MIT Energy Initiative), I was never directly involved in any of them. How does one transition from a mere observer to the builder of a vibrant and sustainable unit within MIT, an institution known for its competitiveness and high standards? I was destined to find out.

Startups within Academia

As at many other competitive academic institutions, the MIT community rigorously evaluates new initiatives. The quality of every program is closely monitored, as is the opportunity cost associated with the allocation of resources to a potentially unsuccessful endeavor. Appropriately, I think, such evaluations take place irrespective of MIT's need for a particular initiative. I often liken the MIT system to a human body in need of an organ transplant. No matter how urgently the body requires the transplant, the immune system will initially resist it once it's introduced. Integration is only achieved when the necessary adjustments align incentives and guarantee that the unit fulfills its promises.

My personal engagement with the committee of 40 faculty members who laid out the blueprint for IDSS was at least as important as their resulting roadmap in helping me shape the results. The depth of discussions, the diversity of viewpoints, the historical context, and the array of arguments we engaged in could never be fully integrated into the final report. Rather, it was participating in all the committee meetings and engaging in countless one-on-one discussions that gave me a profound understanding of our community's expectations.

I must acknowledge that similar ideas and initiatives were being considered or were underway at other institutions. Every initiative was unique, certainly, and each institution tailored its approach to fulfill specific needs. And although I couldn't fully understand from the outside the complex challenges faced by other leaders, I actively sought to learn from their successes and setbacks.

My mentor, Sanjoy Mitter, who was the director of MIT's LIDS when I was hired, frequently advised, "If you surround yourself with good people, you will always succeed." I've been guided by this profound insight throughout my career. In the realm of research, this translates into working with creative and intelligent students who approach their work with good attitudes and into collaborating with colleagues whose interactions are stimulating and exciting. But what does this mean for those of us who are striving to create a new academic unit? And what defines a "good" colleague in this context? Does it mean effective administrators, pleasant individuals, or those who are intellectually strong? What qualities do we need in the individuals who join such endeavors?

Intellectual Strength Is Key

My observations of various department heads and directors at MIT and other academic institutions convince me that the intellectual strength of the leaders is far more critical than their ability to run the trains. This is not to discount the significance of the latter but rather to highlight that strong intellectual capabilities are essential for driving dynamic and groundbreaking developments within the academic sphere. Recognizing that no single person possesses all the skills necessary to establish a transdisciplinary unit that spans various departments and majors, the founding team must collectively exhibit this intellectual prowess. They also must possess sufficient overlap of interest as well as the capacity to interact with a broad range of experts from other domains. My plan was to recruit such individuals and continue expanding the team to fulfill our ultimate objectives.

Working with such a team can be a challenge. By their very nature, they are not a group with whom you can be prescriptive. They must have sufficient autonomy to shape what needs to be done. Accordingly, I took on the role of understanding and coordinating their plans, even when it involved resisting the urge to push my point of view.

Is it necessary to become a psychologist to create and manage such a unit? Perhaps one adopts some psychological insight along the way. A significant part of this role is comprehending the right incentives for each of your colleagues (not just the core leadership group). While an intellectual vision is crucial, it doesn't guarantee continued progress. You must facilitate the engagement of others through funding, student recruitment, research collaborations, structured communication (i.e., regular meetings), and more. Such components help maintain the momentum required to realize shared objectives.

Additional Building Blocks and Obstacles

The question of who runs the trains is also vital. Without the right staff leaders, none of the faculty leadership team's vision can reach fruition. This was one of the most crucial and challenging aspects of my role. While assessing the strengths of my academic colleagues came more naturally to me, hiring the right staff was a different matter. Fortunately, the first few staff leaders who joined IDSS from within MIT embraced the startup spirit, and they enabled us to expand from there. In this realm, as well, I learned that providing a level of autonomy that corresponds to a higher level of responsibility was key. Creating an environment that fostered a startup mentality was critical for team cohesion – and to achieving the desired outcomes.

Much as in the business world, conceiving an academic startup with a unique and promising business model quickly unearths a landscape filled with competitors. This scenario often triggers a perception of encroaching on other people's domains – as well as their value propositions and the resources available to them. Anticipating this circumstance can be nearly impossible. Some of these concerns stem from knee-jerk reactions to something new, while others are legitimate challenges within a vibrant and growing institution. In either case, leaders of a new venture must address those concerns with sensitivity. Successful approaches will vary significantly – no one-size-fits-all solution for such situations – and the complexity of the landscape will compound the challenges facing a team of founders.

Vignette

When examining the proposed mission of IDSS, economics faculty members may have viewed the Triangle as something they were already doing with aspects already embedded in their curricula. We countered that concern by pointing out that economists often abstract away details of physical phenomena that risk over-simplifying the systems piece in contrast to the more complex IDSS approach.

On another front, computer science colleagues had to be convinced that our quest to establish this transdicipline would not impact their brand or alter their role on campus. As we strengthened statistics and reaffirmed our commitment to embed the new ideas within DSS into all domains, we were able to clarify that this was not the role of the CS department.

MIT operates under a system where every degree-granting unit with faculty members is evaluated by a visiting committee every two years. This frequent assessment offers an excellent opportunity to present a unit's progress, challenges, and accomplishments. As far as I know, our reviews at MIT occur much more frequently than at many other institutions (once a decade is more common). Visiting committees comprise MIT Corporation members, external individuals, both industry and academia and presidential appointees – a decidedly unique set of perspectives for a startup such as IDSS.

The visiting committee for IDSS provided immensely helpful feedback and advice that influenced the characteristics of our entity. One natural inclination among committee members was to expand our vision to leverage the ongoing data science and AI revolution and engage a broader community outside MIT. During our founding years, the leadership team held firm to the core mission of embedding our transdisciplinary approach into all academic units in order to systematically address societal challenges. Nine years on, IDSS is better-positioned than ever to pursue its original primary objective –to analyze and solve real-world challenges.

Administrative Duties Need Not Be Limiting

Did I become a full-time administrator? As most academicians can attest, our initial attraction to universities typically stems from our fervor for research and teaching, not administrative roles. When I assumed the role of director for the new entity, some of my colleagues offered their mock condolences. The jest, however playful, highlighted for me the underlying value system in academia. Psychologically, I had to justify to myself why I was taking on this role –constructing a new entity at MIT with the potential to transform research and education.

The endeavor had the qualities of a sponge, absorbing whatever time I allocated to it. My passion for research and teaching remained undiminished, but I had to make the decision to reduce my teaching load while continuing my research. Thankfully, the interactions I had during this period broadened the horizons of my research. After many years in an administrative role, I can confidently report back to my colleagues that I am now more expansive in my research interests and more excited about a wider range of academic pursuits. I've also seen this phenomenon at play in the work of my colleagues, a perfect example of which is the research we've been pursuing regarding systemic racism.

Returning to Ethics

I am not a sociologist or an ethicist, but it strikes me that technology moves much faster than our social and humanistic understanding of its impacts. I find the ethics related to various technologies somewhat puzzling. Would we have dropped a nuclear bomb on Japan if we had had better training in the ethical issues associated with mass destruction? Was it genuinely difficult to appreciate the ethical issues associated with the bomb? Or did utilitarian metrics dominate our thinking? Ethics is a foundational concept from philosophy that I find applicable across the board. But, the debate about whether something is ethical requires a new paradigm where social and humanistic responsibility occupies the same level as economic values in our priorities.

Maybe the biggest impact IDSS had on my thinking is the recognition of the utilitarian dominance of our thinking as we design systems – whether financial, governance, or even social. Monetary objectives drive systems design and push us towards clear economic incentives. Often, such thinking results in gross discrimination and lack of fairness within communities that do not factor largely in such metrics. As the shift towards AI increases, the emphasis on those utilitarian objectives grows. The result is even more biased in the way that the systems we build affect our societies. We see this over and over in technology driven systems such as credit scores, investments, healthcare, or general resource allocation.

We seem to be chasing our tails with such problems. We create efficient, low-cost, low-risk systems that discriminate among people, then we try to undo this effect by tweaking our designs to accommodate known biases. We now see, however, that our tweaks often create new biases. Technology has become a tool for discrimination even as we represent it as combating or removing the biases people bring to their interactions. I love a quote shared by one of my colleagues in political science when we were working on the formation of IDSS. She said, "Engineers and computer scientists look for technology to solve problems. In humanities and social sciences, these solutions are perceived as the problem."

The need for a paradigm shift is imminent. I can't say I know what the new paradigm will be. Economic success, efficiency, low risk, and high margins are all immediate incentives that attract investments. But humanitarian issues are longer-term issues that are not immediate drivers for many market players with capital. To regulate effectively, we must properly assess the short-term and long-term consequences of every discovery and every technology. Could we have anticipated the impact of social media on children, on democracy, or on our general opinions of world affairs? How can such systemic issues be captured before or just in time to prevent the worst of the negative effects they cause?

We're Only Human, After All

Two decades ago, I often joked with colleagues about my research that I never had to think – or care – about people. I examined problems where the objectives were often related to optimality in some precise metric for decision systems (e.g., designing a control system for an aircraft or autonomous car). While I have extensively considered uncertainty in such designs, people often were not part of the decision systems. My work evolved quite a bit in the last decade as I recognized that many critical problems arising in engineering require the integration of human behavior and effects into the design – the networked transportation systems discussed earlier in this book being a prime example.

People, of course, are much more complicated than physical systems. In general, you can't tell people what to do, and they often are not willing to share their objectives (about which they tend to be quite strategic). In mechanism design, we try to elicit those objectives by designing a platform that incentivizes truthful behavior. While brilliant in conception, often it is extremely difficult to create such mechanisms in dynamic and uncertain environments. The domain of behavioral economics remains the most relevant way of embedding people's behavior into the overall design of a system – and it holds great promise as a model for addressing future societal challenges.

This recognition brought me into full alignment with several of my colleagues. Causality must be one of the most critical aspects of statistics. If human behaviors dictate how we adjust our designs, we must grasp the causes and effects of such behaviors. One key advantage of the integration of AI with an understanding of human behavior is the potential to avoid the bias created by human decision-making. We have talked about herding caused by our bounded rationality as decision-makers and by our oversampling of some key past events that may not be statistically significant, which often results in erroneous conclusions about cause and effect. AI systems can assist us by providing a sense of deviation from what appears to be a statistically significant conclusion.

I firmly believe that a systematic understanding of causality will rely heavily on domain knowledge. One can derive so much in abstraction, but the specific nuances of a problem are what ultimately will lead to progress. Causality benefits substantially from pinning down the systemic aspects of data creation – not just in engineering systems, but in many platforms that elicit people's behavior and data. Ideally, that interaction will lead to better platform designs that enable the public to access relevant information. We also can hope that the market for data evolves to include more humanistic standards and objectives.

I continue to be awed by the forward-looking vision of my IDSS colleagues. They understand that systems – right there alongside data – are a fundamental component of the challenges facing humanity. Although I don't see our society shifting quickly to embrace a new humanitarian paradigm, I do see a plethora of interesting questions that can only be answered by technical and humanists coming together – and we are beginning to do so, at least in academia. To succeed, we must be prepared to make major sacrifices on both the technical and humanistic sides. We are tackling challenges that are ill-defined and that do not belong to any clear academic community. We will be required to depart from the tools with which we have grown comfortable and embrace broader perspectives in our research. Personally, I am at that crossroads, and I invite as many of my colleagues as possible to join me.

ACKNOWLEDGMENTS

It often takes a village, and the collective effort of building IDSS was no exception. Numerous individuals played pivotal roles in its establishment. Although I cannot fully express the credit owed to each person, I'd like to offer a few words about some of them.

The 40-member committee responsible for formulating the vision, mission, and structure of IDSS engaged in profound deliberations about the most effective path to success. Although the general blueprint provided a directional guide for implementation anchored in a distinct and vibrant vision, the pivotal role of the founding team extended beyond mere planning. I cannot help but use superlatives to express my profound admiration for this group of individuals – their exceptional brilliance, unwavering dedication, and profound commitment were invaluable. It is an understatement to say that none of the progress we've achieved would have been possible without this remarkable team.

The composition of the leadership team corresponded to various startup needs of IDSS – the development of the PhD program, the launching of the Statistics and Data Science Center (SDSC), the adaptation of the Technology Policy Program, the hiring of new faculty, and the push for related initiatives across campus. Each team member had a profound impact on the outcome of our new Institute.

Our Dream Team

A MIT colleague and friend at once posed a thought-provoking question, "Who is the one individual without whom IDSS would not have become a reality?" My unequivocal response was Ian Waitz, who served as the dean of engineering during this pivotal period. Ian played an extraordinary role not only by enabling this endeavor but also by entrusting me and my leadership team with the responsibility of navigating the complex terrain of creating this new entity. His unwavering support and facilitation were truly exceptional. Among the MIT leadership team, then Dean of Science Michael Sipser played a pivotal role in the establishment of SDSC within IDSS. His perspective on statistics at MIT, his vision for building a robust unit, and his support for the leadership team were integral to the launch of IDSS.

My colleague Ali Jadbabaie is probably the most influential figure in shaping my thinking during the creation of IDSS's vision document. Ali is an institution builder and confidant, and his invaluable insights from his own research and from past initiatives at the University of Pennsylvania were instrumental in shaping the new Institute's direction. Although he wasn't officially a member of the 10-person subcommittee tasked with crafting our vision document, his contributions in absentia helped crystallize many of the group's discussions. The collaborative efforts of this subcommittee, coupled with Ali's personal support, enabled us to articulate a compelling vision for IDSS. When we initiated the project, Ali joined MIT and became an integral part of the founding team. He was involved in virtually every decision, from designing academic programs to selecting the future entity's logo colors. He also took the helm of the Sociotechnical Systems Research Center (SSRC) and our flagship PhD program SES.

My colleague John Tsitsiklis is a thoughtful, brilliant problem solver, a team player, and possesses the ability to see all dimensions of a challenge simultaneously. John initially led the committee responsible for defining the PhD SES program, which included key faculty members from across MIT. Later, he assumed leadership of the LIDS – the oldest lab at MIT – which subsequently became part of IDSS. John adeptly managed LIDS's growth and fostered a harmonious and collaborative relationship between this research lab and IDSS. John's most significant contribution, however, lies in his wisdom and ability to provide candid feedback to the leadership team.

My colleague Devavrat Shah undertook the seemingly impossible task of establishing an SDSC within IDSS. Under his guidance, IDSS unified MIT's efforts in statistics and created several new academic offerings – a minor in statistics and data science, an interdisciplinary

PhD in statistics, an online MicroMasters program (comprising online MIT PhD-level courses), and a professional online course in data science and ML. Devavrat's leadership and unwavering determination achieved what MIT had been pursuing for more than 45 years, a testament to his remarkable ability to surmount obstacles and make things happen.

My colleague Alberto Abadie served as one of the Associate Directors of IDSS and represented the MIT School of Humanities, Arts, and Social Sciences (SHASS). Alberto's dedicated efforts were instrumental in promoting IDSS's vision within SHASS and recruiting faculty to SDSC. He also provided vital support to the SES PhD program, guiding new students in navigating this innovative program. Alberto's research in statistics attracted numerous students to engage in compelling research endeavors.

My colleague Noelle Selin, in her role as the director of the Technology and Policy Program, injected her passion for science in policymaking into leading TPP while simultaneously providing guidance to the team in growing other units within IDSS. Noelle also stepped up to lead IDSS after my departure in July 2023.

In my view, our core achievement at IDSS has been to build an inclusive culture around data science and our new academic discipline. Director of Administration and Finance Jennifer Kratochwill, my chief of staff, played an essential role in shaping the culture of IDSS. Jennifer embraced the challenge of engaging staff, students, postdocs, research scientists, and faculty and fostered a culture of collaboration among our diverse community, most notably the staff. Under her leadership, IDSS services were consistently celebrated as among the best at MIT. Jennifer was also a cofounder who offered critical and thoughtful advice, and her ability to implement decisions was truly commendable. I still hear her voice in my head whispering some valuable advice for dealing with challenging situations.

Our staff played an essential role in the creation of IDSS. Beth Milnes, IDSS's academic administrator, has been the driving force behind our flagship academic offering SES. The program charted new territory in training trilingual students to conduct research that addresses societal challenges. Navigating such a program from the students' perspective can be in itself challenging. Beth has administered this program since its inception with a keen instinct for the student perspective, and she remains dedicated to its success. Beth's exceptional talents and unwavering commitment to the students are major reasons why this program has thrived.

Facilitating collaborations necessitated the establishment of a highly resilient external partnership program. Elizabeth Bruce, who inaugurated this function at IDSS, played a pivotal role in shaping the framework for our collaborations. With her systematic approach to engaging with corporations and presenting a clear value proposition, Elizabeth significantly contributed to establishing enduring external partnerships for IDSS.

Lastly, my colleague Steven Graves played a pivotal role in guiding the entire team throughout the establishment of IDSS. Steve's extensive experience at MIT, his prior leadership of MIT's Engineering Systems Division (ESD), and his thoughtful approach proved to be invaluable assets as we embarked on our pioneering journey.

The Next Generation of Leaders

The sustainability of a new academic unit within a university hinges on the participation of leaders capable of evolving the mission and enhancing various aspects of the organization. A few years after the inception of IDSS, several founding team members transitioned to new roles. John and Devavrat stepped down, Ali transitioned to the department head of Civil and Environmental Engineering, and new leaders stepped into key positions.

Fotini Christia succeeded Ali in leading SSRC and the SES program. It was imperative for IDSS to have a computational social scientist (Fotini is a political scientist) take on a leadership role. Under her stewardship, IDSS launched the Initiative on Combating Systemic Racism, which garnered significant participation from MIT faculty, students, and postdocs. Fotini brought an abundance of energy and enthusiasm to not only this initiative but also to her connections with faculty in the social sciences and humanities. Fotini's exceptional interpersonal skills and strategic acumen were evident in her leadership, and her ability to connect people and her strategic insights made her an invaluable asset to IDSS. Her contributions made her the prime candidate to lead IDSS. Now as the director she continues to branch out and to connect the institute with other units at MIT.

My colleague Ankur Moitra assumed the role previously held by Devavrat in leading SDSC. Ankur is known for his introspective and systematic approach to driving success. He chose to support IDSS by enhancing the SDSC course offerings in statistics during the first two years of student engagement. Ankur underscored the importance of mathematical rigor in applied work and played a pivotal role in shaping the foundation of statistics at MIT that Devavrat had established.

As I detailed earlier in this book, the pandemic presented IDSS with its first real-time challenge and afforded us the opportunity to demonstrate our capacity for addressing urgent problems. We swiftly restructured our operations to support data-driven decision-making. In this endeavor, my colleague Annett (Peko) Hosoi played a pivotal leadership role. Her relentless pursuit of pushing the boundaries of what was achievable and her engaging approach to research elevated IDSS's standing within MIT. Subsequent to our actions, many institutions adopted MIT-inspired solutions for safely reopening their campuses. The "when-to-test" app we developed ultimately found utility in numerous schools and universities, with the National Institutes of Health (NIH) promoting it for broader use. Peko was also a great advisor and confidant for me personally throughout the launch and development of IDSS.

I consider the MITx MicroMasters program and our broader online education initiatives among the most significant contributions of IDSS to academia. I want to express my heartfelt gratitude to Karene Chu for her exceptional efforts in advancing the MicroMasters program to its current state. I also extend my appreciation to all the faculty members who have contributed to the MicroMasters, including Devavrat Shah, John Tsitsiklis, Patrick Jaillet, Philippe Rigollet, Tommi Jaakkola, Regina Barzilay, Esther Duflo, Sarah Ellison, Caroline Uhler, and Stefanie Jegelka. Their dedication and expertise have been instrumental in the success of those programs.

Looking beyond the MicroMasters program, IDSS has been keenly focused on advancing online education to broaden access to AI and ML. Our robust partnership with MIT Professional Education, under the astute leadership of Bhaskar Pant, has played a pivotal role in this endeavor. Moreover, I am deeply appreciative of the exceptional contributions made by the Great Learning team, who have been instrumental in delivering top-tier programs with the support of experts from around the globe. I would like to extend my heartfelt gratitude to Milind Kopikare and Mohan Lakhamraju for their invaluable collaboration in our initiatives.

The impact of the MicroMasters is difficult to overstate. One important consequence is the collaboration with the Brescia family through their social impact lab Aporta. The team at Aporta was simply incredible. I am indebted to Jaime Aroaz Medanic and Luz Fernandez for initiating and nurturing this partnership as well as to Lucia Gonzales, who assumed Luz's role and continues to support the IDSS mission through the MicroMasters program.

Thanks to Many Colleagues

In academia, achieving success extends beyond having a compelling vision; it necessitates the cultivation of trust and garnering of support from an array of individuals. Throughout the establishment of IDSS, I had the privilege of collaborating closely with many dedicated individuals who played pivotal roles in advancing our mission. While I cannot possibly acknowledge everyone, I want to express my heartfelt gratitude to several key figures including former MIT President Rafael Reif, who embraced our vision and encouraged our formation, as well as former Provost Marty Schmidt, whose rigorous attention to the formation and generous financial support were crucial.

Anantha Chandrakasan, who later became the dean of engineering, also provided invaluable support and guidance during IDSS's formation. Daron Acemoglu, who played an instrumental role in shaping the vision of IDSS and later became an ambassador for the Institute in the field of economics. Sanjay Sarma, who led the Office of Digital Learning, played a pivotal role in the creation of the MicroMasters Program in Data Science and Statistics. Collaborations with and contributions from various MIT department heads and deputy deans – Markus Buehler, Evelyn Wang, Tom Mrowka, Ezra Zuckerman Sivan, Whitney Newey, Jim DiCarlo, Asu Ozdaglar, and many others – during the recruitment and hiring process were essential to the development of IDSS. Finally, I owe special thanks to our core IDSS faculty for advancing the broad agenda of this new department.

Our MIT visiting committee played an indispensable role in offering guidance and support to IDSS. I am especially thankful to Jim Champy, who drew on his background in re-engineering to provide invaluable advice and oversight for the transition from ESD to IDSS. Mark Gorenberg also deserves recognition for his pivotal role in IDSS's transition into the College of Computing as well as his unwavering support and encouragement. In addition, I would like to acknowledge the consistent support of Jennifer Chayes, both during her tenure at Microsoft Research and later as part of the visiting committee. Her insights, connections, and encouragement were truly remarkable. My thanks, also, to UC Berkeley professor and researcher Michael I. Jordan for his consistent support of our overall initiative as well as of the statistics effort within IDSS in particular. Of course, I would like to thank my students, as well as my friends and colleagues from my research communities, particularly Jeff Shamma and John Doyle, for 35 years of invaluable discussions that have shaped my career.

These individuals, along with our dedicated faculty members, have made immeasurable contributions to the success of IDSS, and I am deeply grateful for their unwavering support and tireless efforts. Numerous people have assisted IDSS and served on advisory boards, and we owe a debt of gratitude for their valuable contributions.

Securing substantial funds was crucial for IDSS to function as a research enabler. I extend our gratitude for the generous gift from Phyllis Hammer, who supports the SES program, the generous gift from Tom Seibel, who supports a faculty chair, and contributions from the Brescia family, which have funded general operations and fellowships.

I also want to extend a special thanks to Alan Willsky, who served as the director of LIDS during our initial efforts. His vision, guidance, and support were instrumental in steering our team.

Lastly, I would like to express my profound gratitude to my colleague, mentor, and friend, the late Sanjoy Mitter. Sanjoy's relentless pushing of boundaries within academia and his unwavering commitment to maintaining the highest standards were a guiding light throughout this endeavor. Although he is no longer with us, his legacy continues to shape the ethos of IDSS.

As my math-oriented colleagues often express, completing the last epsilon (a small percentage) of a book takes one over epsilon time. During my 2024 sabbatical, I had the privilege of being hosted by the University of Mohammed VI Polytechnique for three months. Those final touches came to fruition primarily, thanks to the exceptional environment provided by my Moroccan hosts Moustapha Terrab, Mohamed Benkamoun, and Hicham Al Habti. I am profoundly grateful for their remarkable generosity and hospitality.

And there Was Robert

During the pandemic, as I contemplated the idea of documenting the creation of IDSS, I felt compelled to organize my thoughts and experiences into a coherent narrative. With Jennifer Kratochwill's encouragement, I reached out to Robert Thurston-Lighty, whom I'd met during the committee discussions about the establishment of the new MIT Schwarzman College of Computing. We engaged in countless conversations over the course of many weeks, and it was Robert's insightful guidance that helped me shape my message and create a comprehensive outline for this book.

Robert's contribution to this project has been nothing short of remarkable. He possesses the unique ability to translate complex technical concepts from the academic realm into accessible language for a broader audience interested in data science. He taught me the art of engaging a diverse community and capturing their interest in delving deeper into this field. He provided crucial insights into maintaining a balance between exploring less significant details and focusing on the most critical ideas – a valuable lesson that has enriched this endeavor.

The pandemic brought with it a sense of isolation, making personal interactions a cherished rarity. Our biweekly meetings, involving Robert, Jennifer, and occasionally Kathleen Thurston-Lighty, became bright spots in this otherwise challenging period. I cannot overstate my gratitude to Robert for his unwavering dedication and invaluable contributions to this project. Without his guidance and support, I may never have embarked on this journey.

Manuscript Feedback

I would like to express my gratitude to several individuals who patiently reviewed earlier versions of this book and offered invaluable feedback. I extend my thanks to colleagues and collaborators Fotini Christia, John Tsitsiklis, and Devavrat Shah for their thoughtful comments, particularly in validating the accuracy of the content and introducing additional perspectives. I also am indebted to Manon Revel for her careful reading of the book. By approaching the material from the perspective of an IDSS student, she provided insightful comments that resonated well with what a new prospective data science student might seek in the field.

I am especially thankful for the extensive feedback received from my daughter Deema, a data scientist at Google who provided a practitioner's distinct perspective. Her written and oral feedback held particular significance as I experienced the role reversal of a father benefiting from my daughter's constructive and incisive criticism.

Many thanks, as well, to Lauren Cowles, our editor at Cambridge University Press. Her dedication to the ideas in this book and to the polishing of the manuscript were essential to the fruition of the project.

Special Thanks to My Family

In my family, the saga of this project has almost ascended into the realm of a recurring joke. Whenever they've inquired about my current endeavors, I'd unfailingly respond, "I'm in the final stages of completing my book." Often, I'd voice my concerns, questioning the worth of a book that lacked intricate mathematical definitions and equations. Thankfully, their steadfast encouragement and unwavering support served as the driving force, propelling me forward during moments of uncertainty and self-doubt. I want to extend my deepest gratitude and boundless love to my wife, Jinane. In addition to her unconditional support, Jinane was a partner and a consultant in the creation of IDSS. Our infinite discussions about the topics in this book undoubtedly shaped my opinions – as well as what we ultimately created at MIT. I also want to extend my deepest gratitude and unconditional love to my children, Deema, Hilal, and Yazeed, as well as my nephew, Taher, for being there with unwavering support in every facet of my life. My heartfelt thanks and love also go to my sister Diana for her support and love and for being there for our family.

I owe my existence to my parents Wisam Abushaqra, who passed away in 2024, and Abdullah Dahleh, who passed away in 2015. Their unwavering support and boundless love shaped the life they provided for us, leaving an indelible mark on my thoughts and actions. During my formative years, my late brother Mohammed was the most influential figure in my life. Although he left us prematurely, his memory continues to linger in my mind and heart. Every step I take is accompanied by thoughts of how he might have perceived it. I dedicate this book to the three of them.

BIBLIOGRAPHY

Abadie, Alberto. 2021. "Using Synthetic Controls: Feasibility, Data Requirements, and Methodological Aspects." *Journal of Economic Literature*, 59(2), 391–425.

Acemoglu, Daron, Dahleh, Munther A., Lobel, Ilan, Ozdaglar, Asuman. 2011. "Bayesian Learning in Social Networks." *Review of Economic Studies*, 78(4).

Acemoglu, Daron, Ozdaglar, Asuman, Tahbaz-Salehi, Alireza. 2013. "Systemic Risk and Stability in Financial Networks." *American Economic Review*, 105 (2), 564–608.

Akpinar, Nil-Jana, De-Arteaga, Maria, Chouldechova, Alexandra. 2021. "The Effect of Differential Victim Crime Reporting on Predictive Policing Systems." *Semantic Scholar*.

Alsop, Thomas. 2022. "Embedded Computing Market Value Worldwide 2018-2027." *statista.com*.

American Highway Users Alliance. 2015. "Unclogging America's Arteries 2015: Prescriptions for Healthier Highways."

Artiga, Samantha, Kates, Jennifer. 2020. "Addressing Racial Equity in Vaccine Distribution" Kaiser Family Foundation.

Austen-Smith, David, Banks, Jeffery S. 1996. "Information Aggregation, Rationality, and the Condorcet Jury Theorem." *The American Political Science Review*, 90 (1), 34–45.

Auten, Gerald, Splinter, David. 2024. "Income Inequality in the United States: Using Tax Data to Measure Long-Term Trends." *Journal of Political Economy*, 132(3).

Bertsekas, Dimitri P., Gallager, R. G. 1986. *Data Networks*. Hoboken, NJ. Prentice Hall.

Bertsekas, Dimitri P., Tsitsiklis, John N. 1989. *Parallel and Distributed Computation*. Hoboken, NJ. Prentice Hall.

Bertsekas, Dimitri, Tsitsiklis, John. 1996. *Neuro-Dynamic Programming*. Nashua, NH. Athena Scientific.

Bonnefon, Jean-François. 2015. "Why Self-Driving Cars Must Be Programmed to Kill." *MIT Technology Review*.

Brennan, Matthew, Bressler, Guy, Huleihel, Wasim. 2018. "Reducibility and Computational Lower Bounds for Problems with Planted Sparse Structure." *Proceedings of Machine Learning Research*, 75.

Brown, Emery, Purdon, Patrick L., Sampson, Aaron, Pavone, Kara J. 2015. "Clinical Electroencephalography for Anesthesiologists Part I: Background and Basic Signatures." *Anesthesiology*.

Busby, Joshua W., Baker, Kyri, Bazilian, Morgan D., Gilbert, Alex Q., Grubert, Emily, Rai, Varun, Rhodes, Joshua D., Shidore, Sarang, Smith, Caitlin A., Webber, Michael E. 2021. "Cascading Risks: Understanding the 2021 Winter Blackout in Texas." *Energy Research & Social Science*, 77, 102106.

Carey, Alycia N., Wu, Xintao. 2022. "The Fairness Field Guide: Perspectives from Social and Formal Sciences." *Semantic Scholar*.

Christia, Fotini, Shah, Devavrat, Watkins, Craig, Han, Jessy Xinyi, Miller, Andrew, Winship, Christopher. 2024. "A Causal Framework to Evaluate Racial Bias in Law Enforcement Systems." *arxiv.org*.

Dahleh, M. A., Diaz-Bobillo, I. 1995. "Control of Uncertain Systems: A Linear Programming Approach." *Semantic Scholar*.

Dwork, Cynthia, McSherry, Frank, Nissim, Kobbi, Smith, Adam. 2006. "Calibrating Noise to Sensitivity in Private Data Analysis." *Lecture Notes in Computer Science* (vol 3876). Berlin, Heidelberg. Springer.

Falb, Peter L., Athans, Michael. 1966. *Optimal Control: An Introduction to the Theory and Its Applications*. New York, NY. McGraw-Hill.

Gerencer, Tom. 2019. "Parallel Computing and Its Modern Uses." *HP®TechTakes*.

Hasuman, J. 1978. "Specification Tests in Econometrics." *Econometrica*, 46 (6).

Hebb, Donald O. 1949. *The Organization of Behavior*. New York, NY. Psychology Press, 1st ed., 2002.

Hill, Kashmir. 2020. "Unmasking the Company That Wants to Unmask Us All." *New York Times Magazine*.

Jackson, Matthew O. 2008. *Social and Economic Networks*. Princeton, NJ. Princeton University Press.

Jadbabaie, Ali, Shah, Devavrat, Sarkar, Arnab. 2023. "Implicit Feedback Policies for COVID-19: Why 'zero-COVID' Policies Remain Elusive." *Scientific Reports*, 13, 3173.

Khamis, Sahar. 2020. "Media Use and Its Anomalies a Decade after the Arab Spring." *Arab Center*, Washington, D.C.

Kusner, Matt J., Loftus, Joshua, Russell, Chris, Silva, Ricardo. 2017. "Counterfactual Fairness." *Advances in Neural Information Processing Systems*, 30.

Lambrecht, Anja, Tucker, Catherine E. 2018. "Algorithmic Bias? An Empirical Study into Apparent Gender-Based Discrimination in the Display of STEM Career Ads." Available at SSRN: https://ssrn.com/abstract = 2852260.

Layton, Roslyn Mae, Elaluf-Calderwood, Silvia. 2020. A social economic analysis of the impact of GDPR on security and privacy practices. 2019 12th CMI Conference on Cybersecurity and Privacy (CMI).

Lipták, Béla. 2013. "Automation Could Have Prevented Chernobyl." *Control*.

McFadden, D. 1973. "Conditional Logit Analysis of Qualitative Choice Behavior." *Frontiers in Econometrics*.

Newton, G. C., Gould, L. A., Kaiser, J. F. 1958. "Analytical Design of Linear Feedback Controls." *The Aeronautical Journal*, 28(572).

Nicolescu, Basarab. 2009. "Transdisciplinarity – Past, Present and Future." *Semantic Scholar*.

Nobles, Melissa. 2021. *Shades of Citizenship: Race and the Census in Modern Politics*. Redwood City, CA. Stanford University Press.

Parrilo, Pablo A., Thomas, Rekha R. 2020. *Sum of Squares: Theory and Applications*. Providence, RI. American Mathematical Society.

Pentland, Alex "Sandy." 2015. *Social Physics*. London, UK. Penguin Books.

Pierson, Emma, Simoiu, Camelia, Overgoor, Jan, Corbett-Davies, Sam, Jenson, Daniel, Shoemaker, Amy, Ramachandran, Vignesh, Barghouty, Phoebe, Phillips, Cheryl, Shroff, Ravi, Goel, Sharad. 2020. "A Large-Scale Analysis of Racial Disparities in Police Stops across the United States." *Nature Human Behaviour*, 4, 736–745.

Piketty, Thomas. 2017. *Capital in the Twenty-First Century*. Cambridge, MA. Belknap Press.

Qiu, Minghao, Weng, Yangqin, Cao, Jing, Selin, Noelle E., Karplus, Valerie J. 2020. "Improving Evaluation of Energy Policies with Multiple Goals: Comparing Ex Ante and Ex Post Approaches." *Environmental Science & Technology*.

Revel, Manon, Tohidi, Amir, Eckles, Dean, Berinsky, Adam, Jadbabaie, Ali. 2021. "Native Advertising and the Credibility of Online Publishers." *ResearchGate*.

Saman, T., Annaswamy, A. M. (eds.). 2011. "The Impact of Control Technology." Available at www.ieeecss.org

Schachter, Steven C., Bolton, Wade E. (eds.). 2024. *Accelerating Diagnostics in a Time of Crisis: The Response to COVID-19 and a Roadmap for Future Pandemics*. Cambridge, UK. Cambridge University Press.

Schrank, David, Eisele, Bill, and Lomax, Tim. 2019. "Urban Mobility Report." The Texas A&M Transportation Institute with Cooperation from INRIX .

Shah, Devavrat. 2008. "Gossip Algorithms." *Foundations and Trends in Networking*, 3(1).

Shannon, Claude E. 1948. "A Mathematical Theory of Communication." *Bell System Technical Journal*.

Sparks, Grace, Kirzinger, Ashley, Brodie, Mollyann. 2021. "KFF COVID-19 Vaccine Monitor: Profile of the Unvaccinated." Kaiser Family Foundation.

Surowiecki, James. 2004. *The Wisdom of Crowds*. New York, NY. Doubleday.

Sutton, Richard S., Barto, Andrew G. 1998. *Reinforcement Learning: An Introduction*. Cambridge, MA. MIT Press.

Szegedy, Christian, Zaremba, Wojciech, Sutskever, Ilya, Bruna, Joan, Erhan, Dumitru, Goodfellow, Ian, Fergus, Rob. 2013. "Intriguing Properties of Neural Networks." *arxiv.org*.

Travieso, Chat. 2020. "A Nation of Walls: The Overlooked History of Race Barriers in the United States." *Places*.

Uhler, Caroline, Shivashankar, G.V. 2022. "Machine Learning Approaches to Single-Cell Data Integration and Translation." *Proceedings of the IEEE*.

Weiner, Norbert. 1948. *Cybernetics: Or Control and Communication in the Animal and the Machine*. New York, NY. The Technology Press.

INDEX

Printed in the United States
by Baker & Taylor Publisher Services